# SKILLS IN
# RELIGIOUS
# STUDIES

Book **3**

S C MERCIER

Heinemann

Heinemann Educational Publishers
Halley Court, Jordan Hill, Oxford OX2 8EJ
a division of Reed Educational & Professional Publishing Ltd

OXFORD PORTSMOUTH NH (USA) CHICAGO
MELBOURNE AUCKLAND IBADAN
GABORONE JOHANNESBURG BLANTYRE

Heinemann is a registered trademark of Reed Educational &
Professional Publishing Ltd

Text © S C Mercier, 1990, 1998

First published 1990
This edition published 1998

02 01 00 99 98
10 9 8 7 6 5 4 3 2

**British Library Cataloguing in Publication Data**
A catalogue record for this book is available from the
British Library

ISBN 0 435 30205 1

Designed and typeset by Ken Vail Graphic Design, Cambridge
Picture research by Jacqui Rivers
Cover designed by Aricot Vert
Illustrations by Nancy Anderson
Printed and bound in Great Britain by Bath Colourbooks, Glasgow

## Acknowledgements

The publishers would like to thank the following for
permission to reproduce copyright material.

Scriptures quoted from the *Good News Bible* published by
The Bible Societies/HarperCollins Publishers Ltd., UK, ©
American Bible Society, 1966, 1971, 1976, 1992 on pp. 19, 62;
Extracts from *The Alternative Service Book 1980* are copyright
© The Central Board of Finance of the Church of England and
are reproduced by permission on pp. 53, 56, 57, 64;
V P (Hemant) Kanitkar, *Hindu Festivals and Sacraments*, The
Author, Barnet, 1984 for the extract on p.10; The Muslim
Educational Trust for the quotes from *Islam: Beliefs and
Teachings* by Ghulam Sarwar, 1992 on pp. 66, 67, 76, 78, 79;
By permission of Gerald Duckworth and Co Ltd the extract
from *Sayings of Muhammad* by N Robinson on p. 72;
Scripture quotations are from the *Revised Standard Version of
the Bible*, copyright 1946, 1952, 1971 by the Division of
Christian Education of the National Council of the Churches
of Christ in the USA. Used by permission on pp. 20, 22;
Routledge for the extract from *The Sikhs: their religious
beliefs and practices* by W O Cole and Piara Singh Sambhi on
p. 90; Extract reproduced with permission from *Buddhism in
the Twentieth Century* by Peggy Morgan © Stanley Thornes
(Publishers) Ltd on p. 46; Reproduced by permission of the
Union of Liberal and Progressive Synagogues. From *Siddur
Lev Chadah,* 1995 © UPLS. Page 548, the extract on p. 22;
United Synagogue for the extracts from *The Authorized Daily
Prayer Book of the United Hebrew Congregations of the
Commonwealth* on pp. 24, 30.

The publishers would like to thank the following for
permission to use photographs.

Andes Press Agency pp. 49, 52, 55 (right), 57, 72 (bottom);
Brian and Cherry Alexander p. 56 (top); Mark Azavedo pp. 10
(right), 44, 54, 56 (bottom), 66 (bottom); Robin Bath pp. 42
(top), 47 (bottom); Circa pp. 6, 14, 31 (top), 45, 53, 60 (both),
69, 70 (bottom), 81 (bottom), 83 (top), 84, 85, 86, 89; Corbis
p. 27; Lupe Cunha p. 5; Eye Ubiquitous pp. 59, 93; Sally and
Richard Greenhill pp. 15, 16 (both), 17; Sonia Halliday pp. 33
(top), 62 (bottom); Hutchison Photo Library pp. 7 (top), 9
(top), 11, 26 (bottom), 29, 34, 35 (bottom), 80; Christine
Osborne pp. 10 (left), 37, 39, 55 (left), 68 (top), 76, 90, 91, 93
(top); Panos Pictures pp. 7 (bottom), 12, 40, 41, 49 (top), 62
(top), 73, 74 (top), 83 (bottom); Ann and Bury Peerless p. 20
(top); Peter Sanders pp. 68 (bottom), 70 (top), 71, 74 (bottom),
79 (both); Travel Ink pp. 4, 18; Trip Photo Library pp. 8, 9
(bottom), 13, 19, 20 (bottom), 21, 22, 23 (both), 24, 25 (both),
26 (top), 28, 30, 31 (bottom), 32, 33 (bottom), 35 (top), 36, 38,
42 (bottom), 43, 46, 47 (top), 50, 51, 58, 61, 63, 64, 65, 66
(top), 67, 72 (top), 75, 77, 78, 81 (top), 82, 87 (both), 88, 92.

The publishers wish to thank Panos Pictures/Nic Dunlop,
Hutchison Library/Liba Taylor, Peter Sanders, Format
Photographers/Judy Harrison and Zefa Picture Library for
permission to reproduce the cover photographs.

The publishers have made every effort to trace copyright
holders. However, if any material has been incorrectly
acknowledged, we would be pleased to correct this at the
earliest opportunity.

# Contents

# Life maps

There are many things which are uncertain in life. There are, however, two certainties in every lifespan – the beginning and the end. Although these two points are definite there are still questions to be asked about them. For example, is birth the beginning of existence or only the beginning of a particular life? Is death the end of life or is there life after death?

People have very different ideas about the answers to these questions. They hold different beliefs about the pattern and meaning of life too. Some people believe that life has a definite plan and a purpose. Others say it is up to us to find its meaning and direction.

To some extent, the pattern of our lives is already mapped out for us from the beginning. There are things which shape our lives which we can do nothing about, such as when we are born, our sex, our physical appearance, our environment, our family and our culture. Whilst there are some things which we cannot change, we are all able to shape our lives to some degree. We can strive to fulfil certain hopes and ideals. We can learn a little or a lot. We can be content to let life wash over us or we can try to make important changes in the way things are going. Of course, some people have far more freedom to make significant changes in their lives than others.

## Discussion question

*What things can prevent people from making significant changes in their lives?*

We can look at life in different ways. Perhaps we can only really get a meaningful picture of it when we have lived a while. Then we are more able to put things into perspective (**A**). When we are very young, life seems to stretch out into the distant future. Nevertheless, there are turning points and milestones which we can see ahead of

**A** *As we get older our attitude to life may change and we may be able to put things into perspective*

us. For example, in school life when you have to make decisions about what you want to do or which direction to take. This means thinking about your abilities, your character, your outlook and aims in life. The turning points in life are often times for reflection and decision-making (**B**).

Each religion has traditions and ceremonies to mark important stages and turning points in life. There are differences in the way the faith communities mark these occasions. For example, Christians celebrate marriage as a union brought about by God. In Islam, marriage is regarded as a contract between two people made in the presence of God. Although there are differences between the traditions they all require us to think seriously about how we live. They also remind us that we have choices in life and they demand that we take responsibility for our decisions and our actions.

**B** *The turning points in life are often times for reflection*

## THINGS TO DO

1 Draw a diagram to represent the nature of human life. It can be shown as a journey, or as a map, in the form of a circle or spiral or a board-game or chart. Use pictures, symbols and words. The life map diagram (**C**) may help you.

2 'I want to be an astronaut when I grow up!' How have your ideas about your life changed? Write a letter to a friend describing the way you see your life now compared to how you saw it as a young child.

3 Do you think that someone in their sixties has a very different outlook on life from someone of your own age? How will their views be different? Will they be less impatient? Will they be wiser in some ways? Will they care less about what their peers think? Write a poem or a story in which such a person looks back on life and offers advice to the younger generation.

4 In what ways do religions encourage men and women to think seriously about what they are doing and how they live their lives? Write your answer as an interview with a religious person from a religious tradition of your choice.

**C** *Some people see life as a journey*

# 2 Hinduism: stages in life

Hindus believe that this life is only one of many. They believe that everyone is an eternal soul which they call **atman**. The soul lives on after death and takes on a new life in a new body. This means that this life is only a small part of a much longer journey.

## Discussion question

*If you believed that this life is only one of many would you regard it as less important?*

According to the Hindu scriptures known as the **Laws of Manu**, human life can be divided into four stages called **ashramas (A)**. These stages are regarded as important for three particular groups in Hindu society – the priests or **Brahmins**, the princely warrior class or **Kshatriyas** and the merchant class, the **Vaishyas**. The stages of life are:

1 the student stage (**brahmacharya**)
2 the householder stage (**grihastha ashram**)
3 retirement (**vanaprastha ashram**)
4 the stage of one who has given up worldly affairs (**sannyas ashram**).

The first stage is a time of learning. The best time for this is when you are young, before the responsibilities of earning a living and bringing up a family get in the way. The second stage in life begins with marriage and taking responsibility for a home and family – being a householder. The third stage comes at retirement. When the children have grown up, there is the opportunity to spend more time in prayer, reading the scriptures or visiting the temple. The **sannyasin** is someone who is at the last stage on life's journey. This involves giving up the comforts of this world, practising meditation and **yoga**, travelling and teaching. Each stage in life offers opportunities to progress on the path towards **moksha**. This is when the soul is liberated from the cycle of rebirth and finds union with God.

With each stage in life there are religious duties (**dharma**) and responsibilities to fulfil (**B**). It is important to fulfil the dharma of one stage in life before taking on the responsibilities of the next. For example, the student should not get involved in a relationship that will distract him from his studies. Finding a marriage partner belongs to the next stage in life. Hindus believe that through fulfilling their dharma they are able

**A** *Some of the stages of life are represented in this family*

**B** *The dharma of the householder includes looking after the religious life of the family*

to purify their existence. When each individual fulfils their dharma correctly then the physical, moral and spiritual needs of the whole community are served. In this way, everyone is able to make progress on their journey towards moksha.

## THINGS TO DO

1 What are the duties of a student? What are the responsibilities of someone with a home and family? Put the four ashramas as headings at the top of four columns. Under each write the activities, duties and responsibilities that might represent the dharma for that stage in life.

2 Look at photo **A**. Write a script in which you interview three members of a Hindu family about the different stages in life and the dharma of each stage.

3 According to the Hindu scriptures, there are four stages in life. How do you see the stages ahead of you? Do you look forward to some more than others? Draw a diagram to represent the different stages you foresee in your life and write two or three sentences about each. Say what you anticipate will be your duties and responsibilities.

4 Divide a page into two columns under the headings physical needs and moral or spiritual needs. Under each heading fill in examples of the physical, moral and spiritual needs of a community (**C**). For example:

| Physical needs | Moral or spiritual needs |
|---|---|
| Enough to eat | Sense of belonging Friendship |

**C** *This young person wants an education. Is this a moral, spiritual or physical need?*

# 3 Before birth

The religious rituals and blessings related to the stages in the life of the Hindu are called **samskar**. Sometimes this word is translated as sacraments. Most religious traditions have a special ceremony to mark the birth of a child. In the Hindu tradition, the first samskar is performed by the husband and wife even before the child is conceived. Once the pregnancy is confirmed (**A**) there are two more rituals which focus on the expectant mother.

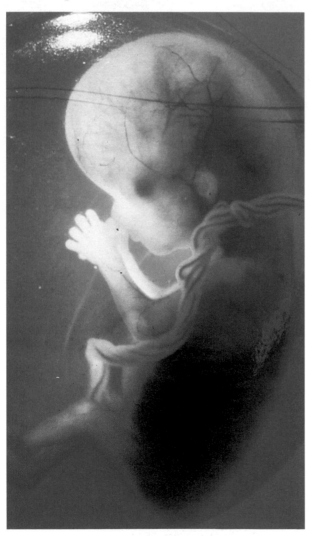

**A** There are Hindu rituals which take place before birth

### Discussion question

*What are the dangers that face the unborn child and what precautions might a mother take before becoming pregnant or during her pregnancy to ensure the health of her child? Do parents have a responsibility to safeguard the wellbeing of the unborn child?*

Between the fourth and seventh month of pregnancy, the female relatives in a Hindu family perform a special ceremony in which the mother-to-be is garlanded with flowers and anointed with perfume and scented oils. She is presented with dishes of the tastiest foods in order to satisfy all her cravings and she is encouraged to try every one. The women sing traditional songs and join together in a festive meal. They wish the mother a safe pregnancy and express hopes for a healthy baby. Prayers are said for the protection of the child at this important time in its development.

During the pregnancy the expectant parents offer gifts and prayers for the welfare and good fortune of the baby at the shrine in the family home or at the local temple. In some Hindu households a special ceremony is held around the sacred fire. This fire ritual, called **Havan**, is a part of many religious ceremonies (**B**). **Ghee** (clarified butter), sweet-smelling incense, such as sandalwood, and grains, such as rice grains, are sprinkled as offerings into the flames.

Hindus believe that the soul is eternal and lives many lives on earth. Birth is rebirth. The soul is simply continuing its journey in a new body. The soul carries with it the **karma** from previous lives. Karma is the effects of actions. Unselfish and generous actions result in good karma and bring good fortune in this life. Selfish or evil actions result in bad karma, causing suffering.

**B** *The fire ritual, Havan, is part of many Hindu ceremonies*

**C** *What hopes, fears and concerns would the expectant mother have for her child?*

### THINGS TO DO

1 Write a letter from Hindus expecting a baby to their relatives back in India. In the letter describe two special occasions – one where the women get together and another involving the havan ceremony.

2 Design a card that a Hindu mother might send out inviting female friends and relatives to come to the ceremony in the home to celebrate her pregnancy. Indicate some of the activities that will take place on this occasion so that non-Hindus who are invited will know what to expect.

3 What will be the hopes and fears of the expectant mother and father in a religious family (**C**)? Write a poem or prayer to express these thoughts and feelings.

4 Some people say we come into the world with a 'clean slate'. Hindus believe we carry with us the karma from past lives. Discuss the difference between these two views. Write up an account of the discussion and express your own views.

# 4 Birth ceremonies

Some of the traditional Hindu ceremonies associated with the birth of a child are closely linked with the important task of washing the baby. This is now carried out at the hospital or by the midwife. In the past, the priest would have done this. Today he still carries out a symbolic ritual cleansing. He sprinkles both the mother and baby with drops of water and recites prayers for their strength and safe-keeping.

Once the baby has been washed (**A**), the mother is ready to receive visitors. Close family members gather to see her and the child and to offer their congratulations.

When the father holds the baby for the first time he may perform a traditional ritual asking the deities to protect the child. He dips a small gold ornament or ring into some honey and ghee and touches the baby's lips with the sweet mixture. He then recites the following prayer:

*'Oh dear child, I give you this honey and ghee which has been provided by God who is the producer of all the wealth of the world. May you be preserved and protected by God and live in this world for a hundred autumns.'*

## Discussion question

*What do you think the symbols of gold and honey might represent in this ritual?*

The naming ceremony takes place on the twelfth day after the birth. The baby is washed, dressed in new clothes and laid in a cot which is surrounded by ghee lamps.

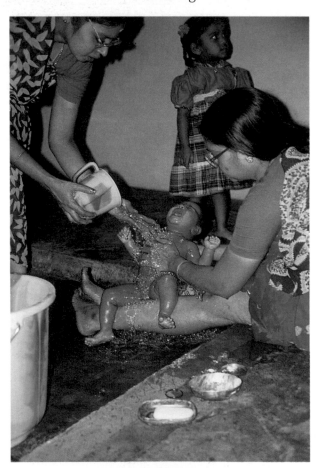

**A** *Some of the rituals are closely linked with the task of washing the baby after it is born*

**B** *May you be preserved and protected by God*

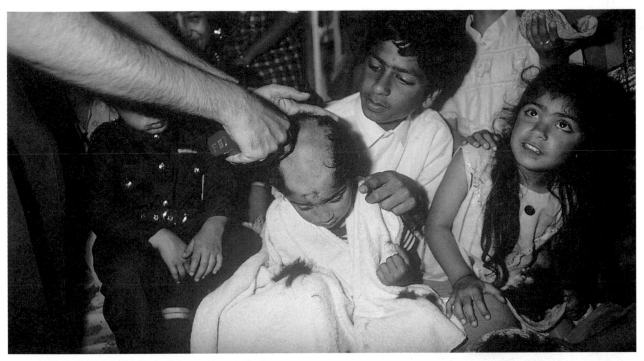

**C** *The Hindu child's first haircut is considered significant*

The priest pronounces the name chosen by the family. It is then proclaimed to everybody present and sweetmeats are shared out. Prayers are recited and everyone sings hymns of praise before joining in a festive meal and celebration. In some families a gold or silver ornament is bought for the child, and sometimes the baby's ears are pierced and gold earrings are given.

Not long after the naming ceremony, there is another simple ritual when the child is carried outside into the sunshine for the first time. This is usually performed by the father (**B**) who holds the baby and recites the **Gayatri mantra** which is the daily prayer of every Hindu:

> *'Let us meditate on the Universal Divine Light, may it illuminate our thoughts and our prayers.'*

Hindu families may also observe other ceremonies during the early stages of the childhood. The child's first haircut is considered a significant occasion (**C**) and the first time the baby takes solid foods is also celebrated.

## THINGS TO DO

1 Write an information sheet on the Hindu ceremonies associated with the birth of a child. Use symbols, pictures and the words of the prayers quoted in this unit to add detail to your work.

2 What are the main hopes, concerns and beliefs communicated through the Hindu birth ceremonies? Explain how these are expressed through ritual and prayer. Give your answer in the form of an interview with Hindu parents.

3 List the special occasions in the development of a young child – from the point of view of the parents as well as the child! For each stage suggest a way in which the occasion could be marked or celebrated to indicate the importance of the event. Share your ideas in class.

4 Write a letter to a friend in which you are a parent expressing the sense of the enormous responsibility that you feel when looking at your new baby.

# The Sacred Thread ceremony

According to the Hindu scriptures, once a boy is old enough to take responsibility for his spiritual education he should begin to study under a **guru** or religious teacher. Entering this student stage in life, called brahmacharya, is marked by a special ceremony when the boy receives the sacred thread. This is worn by Hindu men in the Brahmin, Kshatriya and Vaishya classes (see Unit 2). The **Sacred Thread ceremony** or **Upanayana** sometimes takes place when the boy is seven or eight. However it may be later when he is twelve. It is a sign of a great change in a boy's life.

In the past the young Hindu would leave home and go to stay with his guru who would be like a father and a teacher to him. Today,

few boys leave home in this way as they now receive their general education at school (**A**). They still receive their spiritual education from a guru who may be the local priest. He will help them to read the scriptures, to understand their teachings, to meditate and to perform essential religious rituals. They also learn to develop self-discipline.

## Discussion question

*What do you think is the age at which a young person can really understand their religion and the meaning of its rituals and practices? Discuss reasons why the age you have chosen is a suitable one.*

The Sacred Thread ceremony takes place at the boy's home. Friends and relatives are invited for the occasion. In preparation the boy's head is usually shaved, he bathes and puts on clean clothes. He keeps a fast and can have no cooked food on the day until after the ceremony. The priest prepares by

**A** *Hindu boys receive their general education at school*

**B** *The guru promises to be as a father to the boy*

lighting a fire in a container. This ritual fire represents the presence of God. The priest makes offerings of ghee and grains into the flames and recites prayers to the various Hindu deities. The boy and his father sit at the fire while the priest performs the ceremony.

Before he receives the sacred thread, the boy takes certain vows. He promises to be a good student and to remain celibate (not to engage in sexual activities) until his studies are complete. The guru promises to be as a father to the boy (**B**). He then puts the sacred thread over the boy's head to rest on the left shoulder so that it hangs diagonally across his chest. The thread is made up of three strands joined with a single sacred knot. The priest then recites the words of the Gayatri mantra (see Unit 4) which the boy repeats after him.

After the ceremony there is a celebration and the boy receives gifts from friends and relatives.

## THINGS TO DO

1  In writing explain how the Hindu Sacred Thread ceremony marks an important time in the life of the young Hindu. Say how the tradition has changed over time.

2  Write a conversation between a Hindu boy who has just received the sacred thread and a non-Hindu friend who was present at the ceremony and who asks lots of questions about what he saw and what it all meant.

3  There are several strands or threads that run through our lives, that we rely on to remain the same through all the changes. They hold life together – for example, on-going relationships with family and friends, the daily routines of home and school. Write about the threads that hold your life together.

4  The Hindu boy will wear a sacred thread for the rest of his life. He will hold it when reciting religious chants and when taking part in certain religious rituals. What symbol would you choose for young people to wear to remind them daily of their spiritual and moral responsibilities? Draw or describe the symbol and write a few sentences to explain its meaning.

# Finding a marriage partner

The second stage in life according to Hindu tradition is that of the householder. It is known as grihastha ashram and begins with marriage. For Hindus, marriage is a holy union of two people. It is an opportunity for them to grow together in mind and soul (**A**).

The Hindu scriptures tell of the god Vishnu coming to earth as **Rama**. Rama and his wife Sita are seen as role models for Hindu couples. When Prince Rama went into exile in the forest, his faithful wife Sita gave up the comfort and security of the palace to be with him. During their time in exile Sita was kidnapped by the tyrant Ravana. He took her away to the island of Lanka and tried to persuade her to give up her love for Rama. However, Sita remained faithful and eventually Rama rescued her from captivity. Rama and Sita returned from exile as king and queen. Just as Rama is seen as the perfect husband so Sita is regarded as the perfect wife (**B**). Each fulfilled their dharma (see Unit 2), setting an example for others to follow.

## Discussion question

*What qualities lead Hindus to regard Rama and Sita as the perfect husband and wife? What other qualities is it necessary for a perfect husband or wife to have? Do you think they should share the same beliefs or is this not important?*

Hindu marriage is not usually the result of two people meeting by chance and falling in love. Finding the right marriage partner is regarded as too important to decide on the basis of feelings alone, or to leave to chance. Hindu parents would feel they had failed in their duty if they did not make any effort to introduce their children to suitable marriage partners. In fact most young Hindus are

**A** *For Hindus marriage is a holy union of two people, an opportunity to grow together in mind and soul*

**B** *In this procession Rama and Sita represent the perfect husband and wife*

happy to have their parents involved in this important step in their life.

Usually the parents look for a suitable partner within their own circle of friends and acquaintances. They will want to find someone from a similar background, who will make a good and loving partner for their son or daughter. They will use their judgement to find someone who will be a good and loving partner. They will also take account of age, education and employment. When the parents find someone they think is suitable then a meeting is arranged. If the young person is not happy with the parents' choice then they wait until a more suitable partner is found.

When a Hindu marries, he or she is marrying into an extended family and not just entering into a single relationship with one other person. It is therefore important that everyone is happy with the union and able to give it their full support. Once the couple have decided to marry, the family priest is consulted to arrange a suitable date for the wedding. The girl's family then attends to all the preparations.

## THINGS TO DO

1 Design a cover for a booklet on Hindu marriage using Rama and Sita as symbols to represent the perfect husband and wife.

2 Write a conversation between a young Hindu and a friend in which they discuss different approaches to finding a marriage partner. Make sure you represent different points of view in a balanced argument.

3 Hindu teaching on dharma ensures that the emphasis is on responsibilities rather than rights. Divide your page into two columns using the headings Rights and Responsibilities. Write down the rights and responsibilities of the couple.

4 Letting your parents find your marriage partner does not mean that all ideas of romantic love in marriage are lost. Many Hindus find love – but maybe after the wedding. Write a love story in which a couple grow to love one another after they have been married for a while.

# 7 The wedding

On her wedding day, the Hindu bride is the centre of attention. Her mother, sisters and other female relatives help her to dress and prepare for the ceremony. This is a special time for the bride as she will be leaving her mother's home to start a new life with her husband after the wedding.

In India the marriage is often held at the home of the bride's family, but in the UK the local Hindu temple or hall is usually used. The wedding begins with a simple ceremony when the bride is asked formally if she has agreed to marry the groom. Once she has confirmed her consent the father places her hand into that of the groom. This is a time for exchanging greetings and gifts as the two families are brought together in a new relationship. The groom receives gifts from the bride's family and often the bride receives jewellery. The couple receive presents and gifts of money for their new life together.

The religious ceremony follows. The priest prepares the sacred fire which the couple face, sitting side by side (A). A mark

**B** With each of the seven steps the couple takes a prayer is said

of coloured powder or paste is put on their forehead as a sign of their taking part in a religious ceremony. The bride may wear a red dot (tilak) from then on as a sign of her being married. The priest prepares offerings for the deities and calls on them to bless the occasion. The couple repeat the prayers and blessings recited by the priest and make offerings, sprinkling a mixture of ghee and grains into the flames of the fire.

## Discussion question

*What are the similarities between the Hindu wedding ceremony and any other wedding ceremony you are familiar with?*

In the course of the ceremony the couple are joined together with a symbolic knot. Sometimes a silk scarf is used. United in this way, they take seven steps beside the sacred fire (B). With each step a prayer is said – for strength, health, happiness, children, the

**A** The couple sit together facing the sacred fire

**C** *The giving of sweetmeats represents the sweetness of the union*

enjoyment of pleasures, long life and a close and loving union. The religious ceremony may close with the priest giving a brief talk on the duties and responsibilities of husband and wife. At the end of the ceremony the couple give each other a cake or sweet (**C**). This represents the sweetness of their union and is a symbol of the way in which they will care and provide for each other in the future.

After the religious ceremony is over there is a festive meal and a party with friends and family. In India these celebrations go on for several days with the whole community joining in.

## THINGS TO DO

1 Design an invitation to a Hindu wedding. Use some of the symbols from the ceremony for your design. Indicate carefully the main arrangements for the day.

2 Imagine you have been to the wedding of a Hindu friend. When you were there you were able to ask lots of questions about what was going on. Write an account of what happened and explain the meaning of the events. You can write this in the form of a diary entry.

3 What hopes, aims and intentions for your marriage would you want to express at the seven steps by the sacred fire? Write a poem or a prayer called 'Seven steps' in which these are described.

4 Weddings are times of mixed emotions. There is often a little anxiety and sadness mingled with the joy and excitement of the occasion. A marriage is a serious and important event as well as a very happy one. Think about these ideas and use them to write a short play about a Hindu wedding. Work in a group and act out your play to the rest of the class.

# 8 Preparing for death

Hindus believe that the later stages of life should be a preparation for death. The third stage in life is retirement (vanaprastha ashram). This begins when the children have grown up. Then there is time to concentrate on spiritual matters, to study the scriptures, visit the temple or go on a pilgrimage. In the UK many Hindu temples arrange transport and lunch for their senior citizens so that they can visit the temple during the day. It is often the older members of the community who take care of the temple and who arrange for readings from the scriptures.

There is a fourth stage in life which some Hindus choose to take up. This is the stage of the sannyasin or spiritual seeker. The sannyasin renounces the comforts of home and family and gives up all possessions. They seek to attain moksha, release from the cycle of rebirth and union with God (see Unit 2), and follow a life of self-discipline and **asceticism**. This means fasting, practising yoga and meditation, travelling and teaching others about the path to moksha. No longer attached to this world, the sannyasin becomes freed from accumulated karma and upon death attains moksha.

### Discussion question

*How might travelling and having very few possessions be seen as a meaningful preparation for death?*

Hindus cremate their dead. In the fire the body is purified, destroyed and returned to the elements. In this way the soul is able to move on to the next stage in its journey. It will either attain moksha and be united with God or return to earth to enter another body. In India the **cremation** takes place

**A** *In India a funeral pyre is built near the banks of a river*

outside near the banks of a river (**A**). In the UK a crematorium is used.

When a Hindu dies the body is washed and anointed with sandalwood paste and wrapped in a clean white cloth. Usually the eldest son in the family is responsible for the arrangements. In India, a wooden funeral pyre is erected and the body is laid on it. Friends and relatives gather round (**B**). The son lights the pyre and follows the guidance of the priest in making offerings of ghee and incense into the flames. He recites prayers to various deities from the words of the scriptures:

*'Dear departed one, may your sight return to the sun and your soul be released – to return to the earth to enter a new body or to enter the realms of light.'*

Later the ashes are gathered and scattered on the waters of a nearby river. Many Hindus take the ashes to the River Ganges. Even some Hindus who leave India will return to do this. The waters of the Ganges are so sacred it is believed they can wash away all past karma and help the soul attain moksha.

## THINGS TO DO

1 Write an information leaflet called 'Preparing for death in the Hindu tradition' for social workers who may have to help bereaved Hindus in the UK. Take into account the religious beliefs and rituals associated with death in the Hindu tradition.

2 In western society many people save up for old age. They take out pensions and look into sheltered housing. How does this compare with the way of the sannyasin? Divide a page in two and using words, magazine/newspaper cuttings and pictures illustrate and explain the difference between these two approaches to old age and death.

3 The Hindu cremation involves different elements: fire, air, water; different senses: sight, sound, smell, touch; and of course different feelings and hopes. It is an occasion that will be remembered. Under the title 'A Hindu cremation', write a diary entry of someone who has witnessed one. Try to communicate the different aspects of the occasion.

4 Hindus believe that when the soul attains moksha at death it is released from the endless cycle of rebirth and is united with God. This is a state of pure bliss and perfect peace. Can you imagine pure bliss and perfect peace? How do other people picture it? Collect up ideas from friends and family to put together a collage of sayings, ideas and definitions.

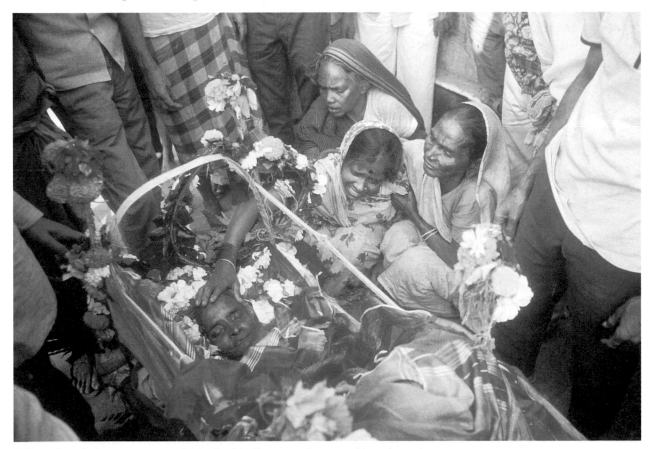

**B** *Dear departed one, may your sight return to the sun and your soul be released*

# 9 Judaism: the seasons of life

Jews believe that all life is given by God. According to the **Torah** (**A**), the most important of the Jewish scriptures, God creates man and woman and breathes life into them. This is described in one of the stories about creation in the book of Genesis. It ends with the reminder that men and women are not immortal but of the earth:

*'You are dust and to dust you shall return.'*

(Genesis 3.19)

Life begins and ends according to God's will.

## Discussion question

*People today believe that they are in control, that the life they have belongs to them. How does the Jewish belief challenge this modern view?*

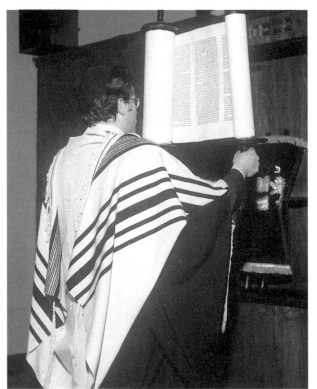

**A** *The Torah scrolls are held up in the synagogue*

**B** *The cycle of the Jewish year is marked with festivals. This is the festival of Sukkot*

The creation stories in the Torah teach about life and God's purpose for men and women. According to these stories, God intended that people should enjoy and benefit from his creation. They were to be responsible and to look after God's world. They were also to grow in number and to build up the human family on earth.

The cycle of the Jewish year is marked with festivals, when Jews remember God's goodness and give thanks for his creation (**B**). There are times of joy and feasting and also occasions for seriousness and repentance.

In the same way, there are celebrations for the different seasons of life. According to the teachings of the Torah, human life begins at birth. In the Jewish tradition, the birth of a child is marked with special blessings. When a young Jewish person comes of age at thirteen the occasion is celebrated with a service at the synagogue. Marriage is the beginning of another new season in life and it is marked by a ceremony which takes place under a canopy

**C** *The huppah is a symbol of the togetherness of a couple*

called a **huppah** (C). When a person dies there are important rites to observe and prayers to be said.

Important occasions in the life of the individual are important in the life of the Jewish community, too. Celebrations and ceremonies bring people together, the community is strengthened and the faith is renewed. The traditions of the community are handed down and the teachings of the Jewish faith are put into the context of daily life.

## THINGS TO DO

1 According to the story of Adam and Eve in the Jewish Bible, men and women will not live forever. Do you think that you would like to live for ever? What would be the advantages and disadvantages? Discuss this in class and then write your own answer to this question.

2 The story of Adam and Eve reminds men and women that they are made from the dust or soil of the earth. What are we made of? Write a diary entry or a story which reflects on this question of what we are made of.

3 What are the different seasons of life? Use symbols, pictures, cuttings and words to make a poster on this topic.

4 According to the Jewish tradition, every occasion in life is a time to remember God and his goodness. There are, for example, blessings to be said when tasting food, others for the new fruits of the season, and there are prayers before setting out on a journey. Take one week in your life and identify particular times when you might express a sense of gratitude or feel like having a moment's celebration. Write out ten such occasions and say how you might express your feelings in each case.

# 10 The path to holiness

The way in which the seasons of life are marked in the Jewish tradition can be traced back to the story in the Torah about the **Covenant**, or agreement, between God and the people of Israel. When God promised that he would take care of his people, they, in turn, promised to keep God's law and follow his commandment:

> *'You shall be holy, for I the Lord your God am holy.'*
>
> (Leviticus 19.1)

For Jews, every occasion in life is an opportunity to fulfil this commandment. Every stage and season can be a step towards becoming holy.

According to the Jewish tradition a person has two opposing inclinations: the one towards good and the other towards selfishness or evil. The ceremonies and celebrations in Judaism are intended to encourage people towards goodness and the fulfilment of God's commandment. They also become holy by performing acts of kindness and charity.

### Discussion question

*What do you understand by the word 'holy'? What activities might lead to someone becoming holy from the point of view of a religious believer? How might a person who is not religious translate the meaning of 'becoming holy'?*

In the first story of creation in the book of Genesis man and woman are told to:

> *'Have many children so that your descendants will live all over the earth.'*
>
> (Genesis 1.28)

**A** *Having a family is a way of fulfilling God's purpose*

According to the teachings of the Torah, having children is a way of fulfilling God's purpose (**A**). It marks a new season in life and is an opportunity for learning to become holy. When a child is born into a Jewish family the words of a blessing are said, as in this prayer for a new daughter:

> *'We praise you, Eternal God, Sovereign of the Universe, that you have kept us alive, sustained us, and have brought us to this season.'*

There are different rituals for boys and girls in **Orthodox** Jewish tradition. Following the birth of a baby girl, the father may be called up at the reading of the Torah in the **synagogue** to recite the blessings (**B**). This is an honour often given in Orthodox communities. Prayers are said for the welfare of the baby, her name is pronounced and a special prayer is said expressing the hope that she will grow to follow the teachings of the Torah.

In some Jewish communities, the women have their own ceremonies to celebrate the birth of a girl (**C**). Prayers and readings are taken from the Jewish scriptures to give thanks to God and to welcome the baby girl into the community.

A Jewish child is given a Hebrew name. The name of a late relative is often taken for the first name. The surname is taken from the

**B** *Following the birth of daughter, the father may be called up to read in the synagogue*

father. Every child born of a Jewish mother is Jewish. The status of the individual as Jew is therefore passed down through the woman. The family identity is given through the father.

**C** *In some communities, Jewish women have their own ceremonies on arrival of a baby girl*

## THINGS TO DO

1 Write three or four sentences on each of the following in the Jewish tradition:
   - the commandment to become holy
   - the inclination towards good and evil
   - the birth of a daughter
   - naming a child.
2 One of the first commandments given to men and women in the Jewish scriptures is to have children. Write a letter to a friend who is Jewish in which you discuss your views and feelings about having a family.
3 Jews believe there is an inclination towards both good and evil in everyone. Represent this view in a drawing or diagram. Explain your diagram and say how it might help us to understand human nature.
4 When a couple have a child nothing is ever the same again – it is no wonder the Jewish prayer speaks of a new season in life. Write a magazine article to prepare couples for this new season and the changes a child will bring.

# Brit Milah

According to the Torah, every Jewish boy must be circumcised on the eighth day after he is born, as a sign of God's agreement with the Jews. This commandment is echoed in the words of the prayer said at the ceremony of **circumcision**:

*'Blessed are You, Lord our God, King of the Universe, who has sanctified us with His commandments, and has commanded us to bring our sons into the Covenant of our father Abraham.'*

**Brit Milah** means the 'covenant of cutting'. Circumcision is the cutting and removal of the foreskin on the boy's penis. This simple operation is carried out by a highly trained **mohel** (**A**). Circumcision is regarded as so important it is rarely postponed. Even if it is **Shabbat**, the commandment of circumcision, must be kept. Only if the baby is unwell is Brit Milah delayed.

At Brit Milah, the father, the mohel and the **sandek** are present. The sandek is a male relative or friend who holds the baby during the ceremony. Other members of the family may also be invited. The mother does not attend the ceremony itself. However she will be present at the festivities afterwards.

There is always an empty chair at Brit Milah (**B**). This belongs to the prophet Elijah who is symbolically present at the ceremony as a witness to the keeping of the Covenant. The father does not hold the

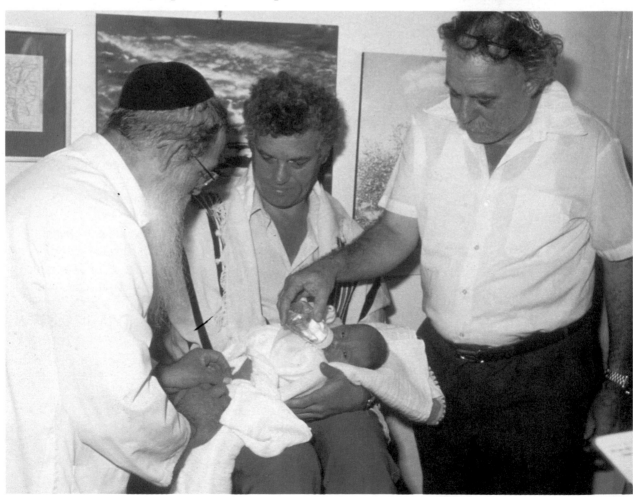

**A** *Circumcision is a sign of God's covenant with Jews*

B *An empty chair is left for the prophet Elijah at Brit Milah*

### THINGS TO DO

1 There is much misunderstanding and ignorance about the Jewish practice of circumcision. Write a leaflet about 'Brit Milah: Jewish circumcision' to explain the ceremony and its meaning.

2 Write a set of questions and answers about Brit Milah in the form of a conversation between a Jewish child and the sandek or the mohel at the family gathering after a circumcision.

3 Brit Milah reminds Jews about important events in the history of the Jewish people. Are there times in school or family life or on TV when you are reminded of important occasions in the past? Draw up a time line of events from the past which still influence your life and your thinking today. Some of these may be personal, some may be of more universal importance.

4 Brit Milah is a time of mixed emotions for the mother and father. Parents have their emotions challenged at many times in the life of a child. Write a poem or diary entry from the point of view of a parent which expresses this experience of both pain and pleasure in raising a child.

child during the ceremony but he recites the blessings. Once the circumcision has been performed someone dips their finger in sweet red wine to give a taste to the baby. Later, relatives and friends are invited for a celebration meal at the family home (**C**).

### Discussion question

*Wine is an important part of many Jewish ceremonies. What do you think wine represents?*

Circumcision is a mark of the Covenant originally made between God and Abraham. It is an outward sign but it is a personal one. To the Jews this is symbolic of the Covenant requiring a personal response. Circumcision does not make a boy Jewish. He is born Jewish. Nevertheless, it represents a link with the very first Jews and Abraham, the father of the faith.

C *Family and friends celebrate after the ceremony*

# 12 Bar Mitzvah

**B**ar Mitzvah means 'Son of the Commandment'. A Jewish boy becomes Bar Mitzvah when he reaches the age of thirteen and one day. From then on he is regarded as an adult in the Jewish community.

## Discussion question

*In what ways do we acknowledge and mark the beginning of adulthood under UK law? At what ages does the young person take on new responsibilities?*

Before he becomes Bar Mitzvah, the Jewish boy attends classes given by the **rabbi** at the synagogue to prepare him for his new responsibilities as an adult in the Jewish community (**A**). He is taught to wear **tefillin** and **tallit** for weekday prayers and he has to study the scriptures and the history of the Jewish people.

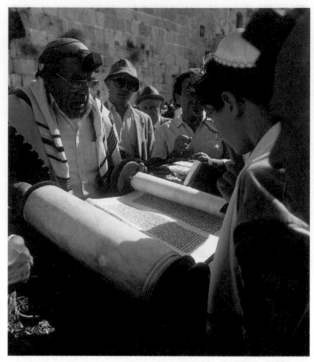

**B** *Some Jewish boys travel to Israel for their Bar Mitzvah. This boy is reading from the Torah Scrolls at the Western Wall in Jerusalem*

**A** *A Bar Mitzvah boy studying with the rabbi*

Some Jewish children attend Jewish schools where they are able to receive their religious education alongside their academic education. Here the boys are prepared for Bar Mitzvah in school hours.

In the weeks leading up to his Bar Mitzvah, the Jewish boy learns to recite a passage from the Torah. This will be the reading for the day on which the Bar Mitzvah is celebrated (**B**). Having attended Hebrew classes from an early age, he will be able to read the text. However he will have to learn to chant the words for the synagogue service. He will also receive careful instruction on its meaning.

The Jewish boy is usually called to read from the scrolls of the Torah at the synagogue on the Saturday morning following his thirteenth birthday. It is a public service when there is a congregation present and family friends are invited. At the point in the service when the Torah is read, the boy is called up to the platform called a **bimah**. From here he will chant the reading for the day in Hebrew.

When the boy has completed the reading his father says:

*'Blessed is he who has released me from responsibility for this child.'*

From then on it is the boy's responsibility to follow the teachings of the Torah and to take care of his own religious education. As an adult in the community he will be able to make up the **minyan**, the correct number for worship at the synagogue.

When the service in the synagogue is over the family and friends usually gather for a celebration (**C**) and the boy receives congratulations and presents from them.

## THINGS TO DO

1 Write an account of a Bar Mitzvah for a local Jewish newsletter. Use it as an opportunity to emphasize the religious significance of the occasion for the Jewish boy.

2 Bar Mitzvah marks a turning point for the parents as well as the young person. Write up an interview with Jewish parents in which you discuss the changes in responsibilities and the hopes and concerns of parents at this stage in their child's development.

3 'If you have learned much Torah, do not congratulate yourself, for that is why you were created.' These are the words of a famous rabbi. What is the message for young people growing up in the Jewish tradition? Do you think that young people should take learning seriously? Design a poster to encourage a positive attitude to study among young people.

4 The celebration of Bar Mitzvah is not mentioned in the scriptures, yet it is a popular occasion in most Jewish communities. Why do you think that growing up is regarded by so many as something to celebrate? Write a song or poem which expresses the importance of celebrating this special stage in life.

**C** *After the synagogue service family and friends gather for a celebration*

# 13 Bat Mitzvah

Today's Bar Mitzvah ceremony for Jewish boys appears to have developed during or after the thirteenth century. The ceremony of **Bat Mitzvah** is an even more recent development. Bat Mitzvah means 'Daughter of the Commandment'. As there are no traditional guidelines for this occasion it may be marked differently from synagogue to synagogue.

A Jewish girl becomes Bat Mitzvah at the age of twelve and the service in the synagogue is usually held on or after her twelfth birthday. Sometimes it is conducted for a group of girls all reaching this age at about the same time.

Those who are celebrating Bat Mitzvah usually read a passage from the Jewish scriptures (**A**). In an Orthodox synagogue this is not from the scrolls of the Torah but a text from another part of the Jewish Bible or **Tenakh**. (The Tenakh contains the Torah, the Prophets and the Writings.) Friends and relatives attend the service.

Afterwards there may be a celebration or party but it is usually not on the same scale as a Bar Mitzvah celebration.

## Discussion question

*What are the similarities and differences between the celebration of Bar Mitzvah and the celebration of Bat Mitzvah. (Look back to Unit 12 to help you.)*

Like Jewish boys, many Jewish girls attend lessons in Hebrew at the synagogue. They learn to read the scriptures and become familiar with the history and traditions of their faith. Jewish girls also learn how to keep the **kosher** food laws and how to prepare for Shabbat and the other religious festivals. Of course these lessons are best learnt in the home where the Jewish mother passes on the religious traditions (**B**).

Jewish women have to keep the same commandments as Jewish men with a few exceptions. For example, women do not have to wear the tefillin or the tallit for prayer. In Orthodox communities these differences have been maintained. It has been argued

**A** *At her Bat Mitzvah the Jewish girl reads a text from the scriptures*

**B** *Young Jewish girls learn of the traditions of the faith from their mothers*

that this is because women are by nature more self-disciplined and inclined to keep the faith. They do not need the same ritual reminders that the men need to encourage them in their religious duties. However, in some Jewish communities the women have chosen to take on some of the ritual practices that were traditionally only for Jewish men.

For the young people involved, Bat Mitzvah, like Bar Mitzvah, is a time for reflecting on the new responsibilities that come with growing up. At Bat Mitzvah the Jewish girl becomes responsible for keeping the Jewish faith and following the commandments.

## THINGS TO DO

1 Write a conversation between a Jewish girl and a non-Jewish friend in which the Jewish girl describes the occasion of her Bat Mitzvah and talks about what it means for her.

2 Design a card which relatives and friends of a Jewish girl might give her on her Bat Mitzvah. In your design indicate some of the new responsibilities that the young person takes on at this time. Use the pictures and text to help you.

3 Learning the moral and spiritual teachings from the wisdom of prophets and religious teachers is an important part of the young person's growing up in a religious faith. What essential wisdom, what moral and spiritual teachings should a young person in a non-religious environment know about? Write your answer in the form of a magazine article for young people.

4 Taking responsibility for your own spiritual life is recognized as an important step in the world's religious traditions. Young people who do not grow up in a religious environment do not have this responsibility pointed out to them in quite the same way. Describe a special ceremony in which this important step in life is recognized for those choosing a non-religious path in life. What would be said on this occasion and who would be involved in the ceremony?

# Marriage

According to Jewish tradition, the union of man and woman in marriage and the creation of a family is a way in which the couple can share in the ongoing process of God's creation on earth. Marriage is also recognized as an opportunity to become holy as God commanded (see Unit 10). Marriage brings joy, security and comfort, and is therefore to be celebrated. It is also to be entered into in all seriousness. Some Jewish couples fast on the day of their wedding until after the ceremony.

In the Jewish tradition marriage is an agreement or contract between two people. It is described as 'a covenant of love and companionship, of peace and friendship'. A marriage document called the **ketubah** sets down the obligations and duties of the husband. This is signed by the groom (**A**). The ketubah is always given as security to the bride. A Jewish marriage can only be dissolved by divorce under the Jewish law.

The marriage service usually takes place in the synagogue. In some countries the ceremony is held outside. A huppah or canopy is set up for the occasion. This is a symbol of the home the couple will share. The bride and groom stand under the huppah before the rabbi (**B**). He begins the ceremony with a blessing over a cup of wine.

*'Blessed are You, Lord our God, King of the Universe, who has sanctified us with His commandments, and who sanctifies his people, Israel, by the rite of the marriage canopy.'*

The bride and groom each take a sip from the cup. The bridegroom puts a ring on the bride's finger and declares:

*'You are consecrated to me with this ring according to the faith of Moses and of Israel.'*

In some cases the bride may also give a ring to the groom. The ketubah is read out and this is followed by the recital of seven prayers or blessings. This is one:

**A** *The ketubah is signed by the groom*

**B** *The bride and groom stand under the huppah before the rabbi*

*'Give these, companions in love, great happiness, the happiness of Your creation in Eden long ago. May Your children be worthy to create a Jewish home, that honours You and honours them. Blessed are You Lord, who rejoices the bridegroom and the bride.'*

The couple again sip from the glass of wine.

### Discussion question

*Wine is often a sign of joy and celebration in Judaism. What do you think it represents here?*

The service ends with the groom breaking the wine glass under his foot (**C**). Some say this is a reminder of the seriousness of the occasion, others say it reminds them of the destruction of the temple in Jerusalem. After the ceremony the couple is given a few moments of privacy. A celebration meal at the home of the bride's family with family and friends then follows. It is traditional for the seven blessings to be sung again, and music plays an important part in the celebrations.

### THINGS TO DO

1 Prepare an illustrated guide to the Jewish wedding. Use the symbols and blessings to add detail to your work.

2 Imagine you have just been to the wedding of a Jewish friend. Write a letter or e-mail to a friend who was unable to attend. Describe what happened and explain the meaning of the ceremony.

3 Marriage is certainly a time for learning how to share, how to give and take, how to put the needs of someone else first. So how might marriage present an opportunity to 'become holy as God is holy'? Write a talk that a rabbi might give at a wedding to help the couple think about the responsibilities of marriage.

4 The Jewish wedding reminds couples that getting married is a serious business as well as a joyful one. Divide a page in two. Under the two headings 'Serious' and 'Joyful' describe different aspects of marriage and married life. Try to make your list a balanced one.

**C** *The service ends with the groom breaking the wine glass*

# A Jewish funeral

Jewish tradition teaches that life is a gift from God and it is to be celebrated and enjoyed. It is the duty of everyone to preserve life. However, when death comes it is accepted and the appropriate response is to acknowledge God's will with the words:

> *'Hear O Israel, the Lord is our God, the Lord is One. The Lord He is God. The Lord He is God. The Lord He is God.'*

Some **Reform** traditions permit **cremation**. In the Orthodox tradition burial only is allowed. The body is treated with the same dignity and respect in death as in life. The Jewish funeral should take place within 24 hours of death. The body is washed and wrapped in a white shroud and put into a plain wooden coffin. There are no flowers or wreaths. Family and friends attend the service at the grave. The rabbi recites prayers and blessings as the coffin is lowered into the ground. The burial ends with the **kaddish**, a prayer in praise of God and his goodness.

Immediately after the burial there is a week of solemn mourning called **shivah**. Members of the immediate family stay away from work. Friends and relatives visit them and bring dishes of appetizing foods. Traditionally all the mirrors in the house are covered. Members of the close family make a small tear in their clothing as a sign of mourning (**A**). Soft shoes are worn about the house and a candle of remembrance is lit. For the rest of the month following the death mourning is less intense but it is still respected by friends and relatives. Every year on the anniversary of the death the family lights a candle in the synagogue and recites the kaddish. This day of remembrance is called the **yahrzeit** (**B** and **C**).

## Discussion question

*What do you think is the reason for or meaning of each of the signs of mourning?*

**A** *Immediately after the funeral there is a period of intense mourning for close relatives*

**B** *Every year on the anniversary of the death, prayers are said*

The teaching of the Torah is that the body returns to dust after death. The spirit returns to its source which is God. Some Jews believe in a life after death. Others look to a future resurrection in the **Messianic Age** when God's reign will be established on earth. Others prefer to say we do not know what happens after death and that such things are best left to God.

## THINGS TO DO

1 Write a set of questions and answers on the Jewish funeral and Jewish beliefs about life and death. You could write this as an interview for a religious TV or radio broadcast.

2 Mourning and remembering are important ways of showing love and respect for those who have died. They also help people come to terms with the loss of a loved one. Write an illustrated leaflet about the ways in which Jews mourn and remember the dead.

3 There is no teaching in the Torah about life after death. This is why many Jews believe it is not intended that human beings should be concerned about the matter. Is this a sensible attitude to have? Talk about this question in class and write up the main points of the discussion. Include your own views on the matter.

4 'I do not want to have to keep telling everyone what has happened.' In today's world the traditional time for mourning is often neglected. Those who have no religious tradition lack the symbols and customs that tell others what is going on. Invent, describe and explain a set of customs, signs and symbols for a period of mourning for people who do not belong to a religious tradition.

**C** *A candle is lit on the anniversary of the death of a loved one*

# Buddhism: outlook on life

There are different ways of looking at life. Some people speak of it as a journey with different stages along the way. Others see it as a gift from God to be celebrated and lived to the full. The Buddhist view of life is influenced by three important teachings of the Buddha.

## Discussion question

*'Life is not a bowl of cherries.' What sayings have you heard about life? Which do you think are particularly apt?*

**A** *Is it true that all life is unsatisfactory?*

The first teaching that is essential to the Buddhist outlook on life is about **rebirth**. Buddhists believe that we are all involved in an eternal cycle of life, death and rebirth. After death we are reborn and existence continues in another life in another body (see Unit 17). There is no end to this process.

A second teaching that shapes the Buddhist outlook on life is the first of the **Four Noble Truths**. This key to the Buddha's teaching is that 'All life is suffering' (**dukkha**). This is sometimes translated as 'All life is unsatisfactory or imperfect' (**A**). The Buddha taught his followers that the reason we cannot find lasting happiness or satisfaction in life is because we are always wanting or craving things (**B**). This craving is like a burning flame. The aim of the

## Four Noble Truths

1. Life is unsatisfactory and full of suffering

2. We suffer in this way because we are always wanting

3. The answer to the problem is to stop the craving

4. The way to stop the craving is to follow 'the middle path'

**B** *We cannot find lasting happiness because we are always wanting things*

Buddhist is to put an end to the craving and to attain **Nibbana**, or the state of perfect peace, when the flame is blown out. Nibbana is liberation from the cycle of rebirth.

The third important key to the Buddhist view of life is the teaching that there is no permanent or unchanging self or soul. This is the doctrine of 'non-self' (**anicca**). According to the teachings of the Buddha there is no soul or self that survives death or continues from one life to the next. It is consciousness that continues. Buddhism teaches that one of the great mistakes we all make in life is to talk about 'me', 'my life', 'myself' and 'mine' as if there were a permanent self which has an existence of its own. This sense of a permanent self makes us cling to and crave the things of this world (**C**). It is this craving that brings us back again and again into existence. If we give up the idea of the self we will see life differently and stop craving. However, Buddhism accepts that most people will talk about a self in day-to-day life.

Most rites of passage in religious traditions are clearly celebrating important moments in the life of an individual. The teaching that there is no permanent soul or self in Buddhism means that there is less emphasis on ceremonies that focus on the individual.

## THINGS TO DO

1 Write a summary of the beliefs about life and death and suffering that underlie the Buddhist outlook on life.

2 How many times today have you used the words 'me', 'mine' 'my...'? Write down as many examples as possible using speech bubbles round the sides of a page. In the middle explain the Buddhist teaching of anicca.

3 Life is unsatisfactory, life is suffering and imperfect. These are illustrated in the photos. Describe each photo and say whether the image challenges or supports the Buddha's teaching.

4 The media and advertising encourage everyone to want and to own things for themselves – for example, a luxury car, a swimming pool or expensive clothes. Design a poster using collage and magazine cuttings to challenge this view of the importance of possessions and its emphasis on selfishness. Use the Buddhist beliefs explained in this unit as a starting point.

**C** *Even wealth and possessions do not guarantee happiness*

# Rites of passage

Some of the ceremonies and rites of passage that mark the turning points of life in other religious traditions do not appear in Buddhism. For example, there is no traditional Buddhist marriage ceremony, nor is there a rite of passage to mark the birth of a child.

The aim of the Buddhist is to reach Nibbana. According to Theravada Buddhism, which is considered the tradition closest to early Buddhist practice, the way to Nibbana is to follow the **Eightfold Path**. These are the guidelines for life taught by Gotama Buddha. The best way to keep to the Eightfold Path is to enter the **Sangha**, which is the community of Buddhist monks and nuns called **bhikkhus** and **bhikkhunis**. These people give up the the kind of life that revolves around marriage, raising a family and running a household. They study and pray and teach people about Buddhism. Traditionally there were no religious ceremonies for celebrating marriage or birth in Buddhism because members of the Sangha did not get married or have children.

The Buddhist community is made up of two groups of people: the Sangha and the **lay community**. Lay Buddhists belong to the world where people earn a living, marry, have children and lead everyday lives. They help to support the Sangha community by giving them **alms** such as gifts of food (**A**).

In the lay community, local beliefs and customs shape the way in which occasions such as birth and marriage are marked. For example, in some Buddhist countries, when

## The Eightfold Path

1. Right Understanding

2. Right Thought

3. Right Speech

4. Right Action

5. Right Livelihood

6. Right Effort

7. Right Mindfulness

8. Right Concentration

**A** *The bhikkhus and bhikkhunis rely on the lay community for alms*

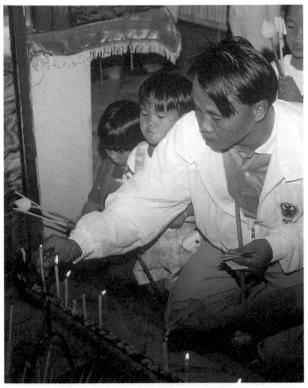

**B** *When a child is born the family make offerings at a local shrine to give thanks and to pray for their wellbeing*

a child is born, the family makes offerings to local traditional gods and goddesses and asks them to ward off evil (**B**). They may also go to the temple (**vihara**) to receive blessings from the monks. Although marriage is not usually a part of the life of those who belong to the Sangha, Buddhism recognizes the importance of a supportive home and family for members of the lay community. In the UK some Buddhist centres are beginning to respond to the demand from the lay community for a religious ceremony to celebrate the birth of a child. In some cases parents bring the child to the temple and make offerings at the shrine.

## Discussion question

*Why do you think that lay Buddhists in the UK are asking for a special ceremony to celebrate the birth of a child?*

However, the teachings of Buddhism say that birth brings suffering and imperfection – all life is suffering and imperfect. From this point of view birth is therefore not really something to celebrate, although many Buddhists will hold a family celebration.

In the Buddhist tradition birth is not simply birth but rebirth. Life is an endless cycle of becoming. Our senses make us desire and want satisfaction. Our desires generate action. Every action has an effect. This is called **kamma**. Good actions bring good kamma and evil or selfish actions bring bad kamma. We accumulate kamma which in turn determines the kind of existence into which we are reborn and so the cycle continues. Birth is just a step in an ongoing process.

## THINGS TO DO

1 What is the reason for there being no traditional ceremonies to mark birth and marriage in Buddhism? Give your answers in the form of a conversation between a TV or radio interviewer and a member of the Buddhist community.
2 Birth is rebirth. Explain this key Buddhist idea using words and pictures or diagrams.
3 Buddhist parents seek protection for their children from evil and from the effects of kamma. What are the dangers from which a child needs protection? Are these dangers purely physical or is there a need to protect the hearts and minds of children too? What are the dangers of greed, hatred, selfishness or even watching too much TV? How can children be protected? Discuss these questions in a small group.
4 Buddhists understand that every child enters a life that is a result of past kamma. What are the influences that shape our lives before we are born? Write a letter or diary entry which explores and explains this idea, asking 'What has shaped our lives?' and 'Where were we before we were born?'

# 18 Growing up in Buddhist society

Most parents want the best possible education for their children. In societies where the majority of the population is Buddhist, the temples serve an educational role in the community. Some offer classes in Pali or Sanskrit. In this way members of the lay community can learn to read the Buddhist scriptures. Traditionally, temples have provided the lay community with opportunities to learn about the **Dhamma** (teachings of the Buddha) and to develop their skills in meditation (**A**).

In many Buddhist countries the temples also provide full-time elementary education for children from the lay community (**B**). Some also offer full-time secondary education and even higher education. Of course the temple is always a community of learning for the bhikkhus and bhikkhunis who stay there.

When someone wants to become a member of the Sangha they go through a ceremony of **ordination**. There are different levels of ordination. Higher ordination is intended for those who are ready to progress as Buddhists and concentrate on the quest for Nibbana.

There is another ceremony which is called initiation or lower ordination. This is for lay Buddhists who join the Sangha for a limited period of time and then return to the lay community. Although some temples ordain girls, the initiation ceremony is usually for boys growing up in Buddhist families. In some traditions, Buddhist parents send their sons to spend a few months as members of the Sangha (see Unit 19).

**A** *Temples provide the lay community with opportunities to learn the Dhamma and skills in meditation*

**B** *Some temples provide education for the lay community*

### Discussion question:

*What do you understand by the term 'initiation'. What examples of initiation can you give to support your interpretation?*

In this way the young person receives his religious education and learns the teachings of the Buddha. This time of separation from home and family marks the beginning of a new stage in the young person's life. It may be arranged for the time when the boy has finished his schooling, before going to train for a job or profession, or before he goes on to higher education.

### THINGS TO DO

1 Write an interview with a bhikkhu or bhikkhuni with the interviewer asking about the role the temple plays in the education of the lay community and the bhikkhu or bhikkhuni explaining the answers and giving examples.

2 Design a leaflet or poster which informs members of the Buddhist lay community of the opportunity to become a temporary member of the Sangha, and the benefits of it.

3 Buddhists believe that spending time in a temple helps the young person develop the kind of skills and strength of character that will help prepare them for life. What kind of three-month period away from home and familiar surroundings would you suggest to prepare young people for the life ahead of them? Write a magazine article to promote your ideas on this.

4 Some Buddhists enter the Sangha during the time between leaving school and going on to college or into full-time employment. This in-between time offers a special opportunity for some young people. What would you like to do if you could take a year out between school and work or further education? Write your answer and give reasons for your choices.

# Initiation

In Buddhist countries there are various popular ceremonies to mark the entry of the young Buddhist into the Sangha. In some traditions the young person is dressed in rich clothing like a prince (**A**). This represents the life of young Gotama Buddha who gave up his life as a prince to become a wandering holy man. The boy's costume is later exchanged for the saffron robes of the monk which are provided by the parents or other relatives. They also help him to prepare for his stay at the temple. The family usually takes food and provisions as alms for the bhikkhus and bhikkhunis.

When the boy arrives at the temple he has his head shaved. This represents his giving up worldly concerns. It is a mark of poverty and self-discipline. He then presents his saffron robes to the senior monk and bows before him (**B**). Kneeling on the floor the boy asks permission to become a member of the Sangha. He promises to keep the rules of the community and to concentrate on overcoming dhukkha (suffering or imperfection).

The senior monk of the temple sometimes gives a short sermon for those who are entering the Sangha. He might offer a few words on the teachings of the Buddha and remind them that the things of this life cannot bring true happiness because all things change and pass away. The aim of the bhikkhu is to seek Nibbana, which transcends rebirth and cannot change.

The boy is then dressed in the saffron robes. The monk who will be his teacher presents him to the senior monk ready for initiation. The boy makes a promise to be obedient to the Dhamma and to follow the rules of the Sangha. Once he has made his vows he is accepted as a member of the community. During his time there he receives instruction in the teachings of the

**A** *The rich clothing is a reminder of the life Gotama Buddha left behind*

**B** *The young Buddhists present their saffron robes and ask permission to enter the Sangha*

Buddha and the practice of meditation. He follows the daily routine of the temple, which begins before dawn when the bhikkhus and and bhikkhunis go out on their alms round. Today alms are often brought to the temple.

In the temple there are **Ten Precepts** or rules for living that the young Buddhist will have to keep:

1 To refrain from killing or injuring living creatures
2 To refrain from taking what is not given
3 To refrain from any sensual misconduct
4 To refrain from lying and wrong speech
5 To refrain from taking alcohol or misusing drugs
6 To refrain from eating after midday
7 To refrain from taking part in entertainments, such as music or dancing
8 To avoid using jewellery and perfumes
9 To refrain from sleeping in a luxury bed
10 To refrain from handling money.

## THINGS TO DO

1 Design a poster to illustrate the Ten Precepts that could be used as a teaching aid for Buddhist students coming up to initiation.
2 Using words and pictures, describe the stages of the initiation/ordination ceremony when a young person enters the Sangha. Explain the meaning of the events in this process.
3 Change of clothes, change of hairstyle, change of daily routine – how will these affect the young person joining the Sangha? In what ways are these three things usually expressions of growing up in our society? Write your answer as a magazine article for young people today.
4 The first five of the ten precepts apply to all Buddhists not just the Sangha. Can you add to these five, thinking particularly of rules that would help young people to think about the meaning of life in today's society before they become caught up in the life of earning a living, possessions and material success.

# Marriage

Members of the Sangha do not marry. Sometimes a married person may join later in life when they have fulfilled their family responsibilities. However, they must first have the agreement of their partner before they are ordained.

Although in the Theravada community marriage is not for those who are members of the Sangha, Buddhists value family life as important. It is believed that it brings balance and stability to the lay community. The Sangha can only survive if there is a flourishing lay community to support it.

There is no traditional Buddhist marriage ceremony or ritual. Usually the local traditions and customs are followed (**A**). For example, in the UK a Buddhist couple will marry at a registry office. Some temples are responding to requests to provide a religious ceremony for a couple after their registry

**B** *Buddhist couples in the UK look to the temple for a blessing on their marriage*

office wedding. This is usually conducted by the bhikkhu in the shrine room of the temple (**B**). Although not a marriage ceremony, this is seen as a blessing on the relationship and it provides an opportunity for reflecting on the spiritual and moral importance of the occasion.

## Discussion question

*Why do you think that many people in the UK do not feel that the registry office marriage is sufficient?*

At such a ceremony the Sangha may invite the couple to attend **puja**. This is an act of devotion during which offerings are made at the shrine of the Buddha. There may also be a sermon from one of the monks on the new responsibilities which the couple is taking on. Buddhist tradition recognizes the woman as an equal partner in the marriage

**A** *Usually local traditions and customs are followed*

**C** *In Buddhist societies family and friends take food to the Sangha to mark a special occasion such as this*

relationship. The teachings of the Buddha emphasize the importance of her status in the community. Both husband and wife must seek to follow the teachings of the Buddha in their married life.

When a couple go to the temple after the registry office wedding, they may sometimes invite friends and family to join them. They will take food and prepare a meal for the bhikkhus and bhikkunis (**C**). Later, everyone will join in a shared meal.

The life of the married couple is often too full of the cares of work and family to lead to enlightenment. However, if the couple live by the teachings of the Buddha, they may be reborn sooner into a life where they can follow the path of the bhikkhu or bhikkhuni and progress more rapidly towards Nibbana.

### THINGS TO DO

1 Write a summary of the way in which Buddhist traditions are developing in response to demands for a ceremony to mark marriage.

2 Design a card inviting friends and family to a ceremony at the temple for a Buddhist couple in the UK following their registry office wedding. Inside the card make sure you inform people of what will be taking place and say how they can help with the arrangements for the shared meal.

3 What are the cares of work and family that face most couples getting married? What can a Buddhist couple do to ensure that their religious life does not get lost among these cares and concerns? Write your answer in the form of a short sermon that might be appropriate for a Buddhist ceremony after a registry office wedding.

4 In most Buddhist temples, those who become members of the Sangha give up married life and all its advantages and comforts. Do you think this is a lot to give up? What will be the rewards? Write a letter or a poem which expresses the thoughts someone might have in deciding to forgo married life and join the Sangha.

# Death is not to be feared

Death is not to be feared according to the teachings of the Buddha. Death is not an end. It is only a moment in a series of moments within the cycle of birth, life, death and rebirth. Death is just a stepping stone from one existence to another. There is no permanent soul or spirit that survives death. Only consciousness continues. When one life goes out another begins. It is like a candle, which, just before it goes out, lights the flame of another (**A**).

The **Three Jewels** of Buddhism help to inspire and support followers on their path to enlightenment. These are:

- the Buddha
- the Dhamma (the truth about life and the Buddha's teachings)
- the Sangha.

**A** *When one life goes out, another begins – just like one candle lighting another before it dies*

Every Buddhist also strives to keep the Five Precepts:

1 To refrain from taking life or injuring living creatures
2 To refrain from taking what is not given
3 To refrain from sensual misconduct
4 To refrain from telling lies and wrong speech
5 To refrain from taking any kind of intoxicants or misusing drugs.

Lay Buddhists who follow these guidelines in life will accumulate good kamma. At death they will be reborn into a better existence. They will be a step further along the path to Nibbana. Because of this viewpoint, Buddhists do not fear death.

### Discussion question

*If you believed that you were going to be reborn into a better life after death would you have a different attitude towards death from the one you hold now? How different would it be if at all?*

For those who have chosen to become bhikkhus or bhikkhunis, death may be the final step on the way to enlightenment. If they have followed the Eightfold Path and have lived a life of loving kindness then they will have advanced along the road to Nibbana. If they have become free from craving and have put an end to greed, hatred and ignorance they will be very close indeed to Nibbana, a state of pure bliss and peace. This will mean the end of rebirth, the end of suffering. Death is therefore not to be feared.

Buddhists believe that there are other worlds to which we may go after death. For example, those who have accumulated good kamma may enjoy a life in one of the heavenly worlds. However, they will be born again in this world until they achieve Nibbana.

Mahayana Buddhists believe there are some beings who have become enlightened but have chosen to postpone their own attainment of Nibbana, taking the vow:

**B** *Bodhisattvas are spiritual beings representing kindness and compassion*

*'May I not enter Nibbana until I have brought all other beings to enlightenment.'*

Such beings are called **bodhisattvas** (**B**). They have infinite compassion and kindness and are active in helping others to reach Nibbana.

### THINGS TO DO

1 Prepare a short play or dialogue in which someone who is a Buddhist explains to a non-Buddhist why death is not to be feared.

2 Buddhists are reluctant to describe Nibbana because it is beyond our ordinary experience and it is hard to convey the full meaning of the word. Write an article for a Buddhist newsletter which explains the path to Nibbana. You can hint at the nature of this state of perfect bliss but warn the reader that it is impossible to put across the full meaning of the word.

3 Buddhists believe that what happens after your death depends a good deal on what happens before. Design a board game based on this belief in which the aim is to reach Nibbana.

4 The bodhisattva has infinite compassion and postpones the bliss of Nibbana in order to help others who are suffering. Design a poster to represent this idea of infinite compassion.

# Funeral rites

Buddhist funeral rites vary greatly from one community to another depending on the cultural background and tradition (**A**). To the outsider the occasion may appear more like a festival than a funeral. Close friends and members of the family are naturally saddened at the loss of the loved one. However, in the light of Buddhist belief about death (see Unit 21), there is no reason to show excessive sorrow or distress for the one who has died.

When a person in the lay community dies, the family attends to the body of the deceased, which is washed carefully. In some traditions, it is then laid in a wooden coffin. This is adorned with flowers and in some traditions carried in a procession to the local temple. It may be set down in a prominent position in the shrine room. Offerings of flowers are made at the shrine of the Buddha and blessings are said.

> 'Reverencing the Buddha we offer flowers,
> Flowers that today are fresh and
> sweetly blooming.
> Flowers that tomorrow are faded
> and fallen.
> Our bodies too like flowers will pass away.'

## Discussion question

*Flowers are often important in expressions of grief across many cultures and religions. Why do you think they are used in this way? What do they symbolize?*

When the service at the shrine is over, a senior monk may say a few words to the bereaved and remind them of the teachings of the Buddha on the nature of life and death. The family and friends will have brought food for the members of the Sangha. After the service everyone shares a meal. This is not a time for indulging in too much grief or mourning. There is a hope that the person who has died will be reborn in a better life and progress on their journey to Nibbana. Later the body is taken for cremation, or in some cases burial.

In some Buddhist communities there are elaborate ceremonies and rituals to mark the death of a bhikkhu (**B**). A funeral carriage and tower is built for the coffin. It is usually brightly decorated and adorned with flowers. This is carried in a colourful procession with music and celebration to the **cremation** ground. After the cremation the ashes are collected up. Sometimes they are scattered into the waters of a lake or into the sea (**C**).

**A** *Buddhist funeral rites vary from one community to another. Here the body is being cremated on a funeral pyre*

**B** *Elaborate ceremonies mark the death of a bhikkhu*

**C** *After cremation the ashes are scattered*

### THINGS TO DO

1 Write an illustrated guide to what happens in the Buddhist funeral rites of:
   - a lay Buddhist
   - a bhikkhu or bhikkhuni.
2 Imagine you are interviewing a Buddhist monk on the meaning behind the Buddhist funeral rites. Write a set of questions and the answers you would be given in such an interview.
3 One of the meditations performed by Buddhist monks is to watch the process of decay. Write a description of the way flowers die and decay. Say what can be learnt about life and death from observing this process.
4 Flowers, candles, poems, prayers, music – all these can help people to express their feelings in response to the death of a loved one. Write down the ways in which you think that people should be able to express and communicate their feelings in a ceremony when someone dies. Suggest your own ideas for such a ceremony.

# 23 Christianity: the journey of life

Many Christians see life as being like a journey, giving them an opportunity to learn and to grow in faith (**A**). Christians believe that God guides and supports them through life just as a parent looks after a child. Like most journeys, life has turning points and milestones on the way. These offer important opportunities for believers to reflect on and to renew and strengthen their Christian faith. They are also occasions for Christians to ask forgiveness for times when they have failed, to pray for courage and support and to make a new beginning.

## Discussion question

*Can you think of an example of a time when a milestone in life, such as a birth or death, has made someone think about the direction of their life or make changes to it? What was the effect of that occasion?*

## The story of the talents

There was once a man who was going away and he put his servants in charge of his money. To one he gave five thousand silver coins to another he gave two thousand and to the third he gave one thousand. The first invested the money wisely and earned double the amount. In the same way the second earned another two thousand. The third dug a hole in the ground and hid his master's money. When the man returned he called his servants to account for the money. The first said, 'You gave me five thousand – look I have made you another five.' The master said 'You good and faithful servant. I will reward you. Come and share my happiness.' The second servant said, 'You gave me two thousand – here I have doubled it.' Again the master was pleased. The third servant brought back the thousand his master had entrusted to him and said, 'I hid your money in the ground – here is what belongs to you.' The master was angry and said, 'You bad and lazy servant. You knew what was wanted – why did you waste the opportunity? Give what you have to the one with ten thousand.'

**A** *Christians see life as a journey*

**B** *This painting shows Jesus teaching. Jesus told his followers they must not waste the gifts God had given them*

Christians speak of life as a gift from God. According to the teachings of the **Bible** this gift carries with it important responsibilities. In the story Jesus tells his followers that they should develop the abilities and talents they have been given and not waste them (**B**).

Christians believe that the opportunities that life offers are not to be wasted. It is to be lived to the full and we must use our gifts and talents well (**C**).

**C** *We must use our talents well*

### THINGS TO DO

1 Many Christians say life is like a journey. What would you expect to find on the Christian's journey through life? Design a diagram/picture to show this life. Include things that they could not look to for help and support on the way. Look at the photos and diagram to help you.

2 Tell the story Jesus told in your own words – you could write a modern version of it. Explain your understanding of the meaning of the story.

3 What gifts and talents might a person be born with? A Christian believes it is wrong to let these things go to waste. Do you agree? Discuss this view in class. Think about the issues raised and write a letter to a newspaper which puts across your view on this matter. Support your argument with reasons and examples.

4 The journey of life – is this saying life is good or life is hard? What ideas and feelings does the image of a journey conjure up for you? Write a short story for young children called 'Life is a journey'.

# Birth and baptism

The birth of a child, marriage celebration, death of a loved one, these are times when people think about life and its meaning. The ceremonies that mark these important events are often occasions for members of the community to renew their faith and to reflect on their own journey through life. This is true of the **rites** and ceremonies for birth, marriage and death in the different Christian traditions.

The birth of a baby is a time when the Christian community gives thanks to God and prepares the way for the child at the start of its journey in life. It is also a time when the members of the community are called upon to renew their faith and to reflect on their commitment to follow Christ.

In the Orthodox Churches there are several ceremonies to mark the birth of a child. There are prayers on the first day after the mother has given birth. On the eighth day after birth there is a ceremony at the church when the baby receives its name and prayers are said for the well-being of the child. Forty days after the birth the mother brings the baby to be 'churched' or introduced to the Church. Again, prayers are said for the well-being of the mother and child on this occasion.

To celebrate the arrival of a new baby many churches have a service of **infant baptism**. In the Orthodox Church **baptism** involves complete immersion in water (**A**). Godparents are chosen to act as sponsors for the baby. Before the service of baptism the godparents are asked to answer in the place of the child when the **priest** puts two questions. He asks if they turn away from the devil and all of his works and if they are ready to be united to Christ. These questions are asked three times. Once the godparents have answered on behalf of the child the baptism can go ahead.

## Discussion question

*What do you think it means to promise to 'turn away from the devil'? What will the parents and godparents have to do to ensure the child turns away from the devil and all his works?*

The church is lit with candles. The priest recites prayers.

> *'That s/he may prove to be a child of Light and an inheritor of eternal blessings; let us pray to the Lord. That s/he may grow in, and become a partaker of the Death and Resurrection of Christ our God; let us pray to the Lord'*

The priest makes the sign of the cross with oil on the infant's forehead, chest and between the shoulders. The child is then baptized by being immersed three times in water. As he baptizes the child the priest says 'In the name of the Father and the Son and the Holy Spirit.' After the baptism in water the child is dressed in a white robe and again anointed with oil (**B**).

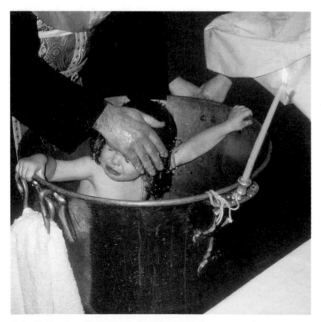

**A** *In Orthodox Churches, baptism involves complete immersion in water*

**B** *After the baptism the child is again anointed with oil*

Symbols are important in Christian baptism. The oil used in this ceremony is called the oil of gladness. Making a sign of the cross is a reminder of the death of Jesus Christ. Christians believe that through Christ's death they are freed from the power of sin and evil. Water is a symbol of the Holy Spirit. The **Holy Spirit** is the living presence of God at work in the lives of those who follow Christ. The immersion in water symbolizes the child dying and rising again with Christ. This reminds Christians that Christ has overcome the power of death. Water is also a symbol of life, especially the new life Christ gives to his followers. Many Christians also see baptism as a symbolizing the washing away of sin.

## THINGS TO DO

1 Prepare a talk on the ways in which the birth of a child is celebrated in the Orthodox Church.

2 Identify the religious symbols in the Orthodox baptism. Design an illustrated guide to the symbolism of the occasion. You should include: light, oil, water and the sign of the cross.

3 Christians regard life as a precious gift from God. Do you think that life is a gift? What kind of gift is it? Is it a welcome gift? Are there times when you have heard people say 'I wish I had never been born'? Do you think they mean it? Write your answers in the form of a diary entry.

4 Choosing the right name for a child is important. What considerations do you think a Christian family may take into account when choosing a name? Write a scene for a play in which a family discusses the name for their new baby.

# Infant baptism

Within the Christian faith there are different Churches and traditions. The practice of baptism varies from one to another, with some baptizing members of the faith as babies, whilst others wait until the person is able to decide for themselves (see Unit 28). The **Anglican** service of infant baptism sometimes takes place during the regular Sunday service. Godparents are chosen by the parents of the child and are invited to the service. They have a special responsibility to keep in touch with the child and to care about his or her religious and spiritual upbringing.

At the baptism, the parents and godparents stand at the **font** with the **minister**. A candle is lit and given to one of the parents or godparents. The parents and godparents are asked to confirm their belief in God and to renew their commitment to serve Christ (**A**). They also make promises on behalf of the child to follow and trust in Christ. It is the duty of the godparents to ensure that the child grows up in the Christian faith.

## Discussion question

*Some godparents are chosen because they are just good friends of the family and have no particular Christian commitment. Do you think that it is wrong for them to make promises in church which they cannot keep?*

The minister **consecrates** (makes holy) the water in the font and then gives thanks to God for the life of the child. Those present are reminded of their commitment to serve and follow Christ. Then the parents are asked to name the child and the minister holds the baby and repeats the name. He or she scoops up a little water and pours it on to the child's forehead (**B**) saying:

**A** *Parents and godparents renew their commitment to Christ*

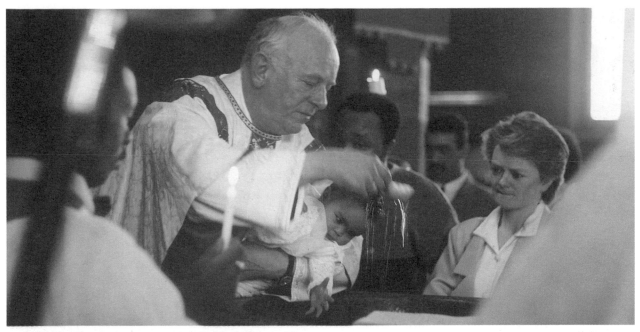

**B** *An Anglican minister pours water over the forehead of a baby*

*'I baptize you in the name of the Father, the Son and the Holy Spirit.'*

Making the sign of the cross on the child's forehead the minister says:

*'I sign you with the cross, the sign of Christ.'*

The **Roman Catholic** service is very similar to the Anglican one, with members being baptized as infants. In both traditions godparents and parents make promises on behalf of the child.

After the church ceremony there is a family celebration at home with relatives and friends. In some households a special christening cake is served. Presents may be given to the baby to mark the occasion.

Some Christians choose to have a **dedication** service rather than a **christening** for their child. A dedication service is an opportunity to give thanks to God for the arrival of the baby. The parents promise to bring up the child in the Christian faith. Later the child may be baptized when he or she is old enough to understand the meaning of Christian commitment.

## THINGS TO DO

1 Write a leaflet for parents, describing and explaining infant baptism in the Anglican Church. Anticipate some of the questions they may have about the service.

2 Write an article for a church newsletter from someone who has just become a godparent explaining what is involved. Give advice on how to prepare and take part in an infant baptism service.

3 Imagine you have been asked to be a godparent. Design a card to send for the christening. Use some of the symbols from the service in your design. Write a message to the parents in the card expressing your congratulations and your hopes for the child's future.

4 Most Christians want to celebrate the birth of a baby with a dedication or baptism service. What sort of service or ceremony might a non-religious person have to celebrate the birth of their child? Describe the kind of ceremony that you think would be appropriate.

# First Communion

In many of the Christian Churches there is a special service when bread and wine are shared in remembrance of the last supper that Jesus shared with his friends. It is called by different names in different Churches – the **Eucharist** or **Holy Communion**, Christian **Mass** or the **Breaking of Bread** or the **Lord's Supper**. In the Roman Catholic and Anglican Churches it is an important part of regular community worship. Usually young children are not given the bread or wine. Taking Communion for the first time is considered an important step in the Christian's journey of faith.

In the Roman Catholic tradition there is a special celebration when children make their **First Communion** around the age of seven. They usually prepare carefully for this occasion. First they **confess** and say sorry for all the things they have done wrong. They must intend to do better in the future. Confession is the usual practice before taking Communion. In his letter to the Corinthians (11:28), St Paul said that everyone should examine themselves first before eating the bread and drinking the wine. Sometimes an individual asks the priest to hear their confession. Many people prefer to make their confession in private prayer to God before taking Mass.

## Discussion question

*What do you think St Paul meant when he said Christians should examine themselves?*

Most children who are coming up to their First Communion attend classes, often run by a priest (**A**). He will explain the meaning of the bread and the wine and the way in which Catholics understand the service.

On the day of their First Communion, the children wear their best clothes, often made

**A** *Roman Catholic children learn about the meaning of the bread and wine before they take their First Communion*

**B** *Boys and girls often wear their best clothes for First Communion*

## THINGS TO DO

1 Write an account of the Roman Catholic practice of First Communion. Explain how young Catholics are prepared for this occasion.

2 Design a teaching aid, a picture or diagram, which the priest might use to teach those preparing for First Communion to explain the meaning and pattern of the service.

3 Christians believe that everyone makes mistakes on their journey through life. They emphasize the importance of confession and repentance. Write a story in which a person finds they are able to go forward in their lives after facing up to what they have done, saying sorry and trying to do better.

4 Roman Catholics prepare carefully for First Communion. The first time we do something is often a time for careful preparation and later a time to remember. Can you remember a special occasion when you were going to do something for the first time and the preparation was very important? Describe such an occasion and say why it meant a lot to you.

or bought specially for the occasion (**B**). The priest invites the children to come up to the **altar** to receive the **host** with the rest of the congregation (**C**). The host is the wafer representing the bread of the Last Supper. When Jesus broke the bread he said it was his body. When he shared the cup of wine Jesus said it was his blood. Christians remember these words when they receive Holy Communion.

In some Churches there is no special service to mark the first time a person receives the bread at Holy Communion. In the **Baptist** Church, for example, people are invited to share the Lord's Supper when they feel that they are old enough to understand and to accept the Christian faith for themselves. In the Anglican tradition, believers do not take Communion until they have been confirmed (see Unit 27).

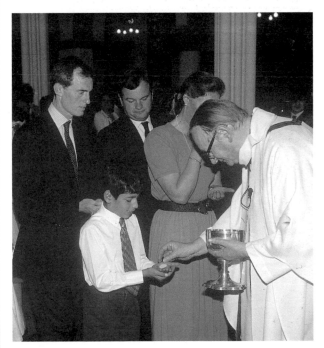

**C** *'Receiving the host'*

# 27 Confirmation

For many Christians, confirmation is an important turning point in their faith journey. The word **confirmation** means 'to make firm'. When a child is baptized as a baby the godparents and parents promise to ensure the child grows up in the Christian faith. At the service of confirmation the Christian makes firm his or her commitment to follow Christ and makes the promises that were once made on their behalf.

The person being confirmed is sometimes called a confirmation candidate. Before being confirmed candidates usually attend lessons given by the church minister or priest (**A**). At these classes they learn to deepen and strengthen their faith through regular prayer, confession, Bible reading, and service in the community. They also learn about the Church and the meaning of the scriptures.

### Discussion question

*What questions about the Church and the scriptures do you think that those getting confirmed might have to ask the priest or minister?*

**B** *Some Protestant churches do not have bishops and the minister carries out confirmation*

In the Roman Catholic, Anglican and Orthodox traditions confirmation is performed by a **bishop**. It is the church minister or priest who leads the service. Usually the theme for the hymns, readings and prayers is the Holy Spirit. At confirmation Christians are reminded of God's gift of the Holy Spirit, who can work through them and give them courage and strength in their journey through life.

At the Anglican confirmation service, Christians declare their personal faith by answering these questions:

- Do you turn to Christ?
- Do you repent of your sins?
- Do you renounce evil?

**A** *Candidates usually attend classes before confirmation*

The bishop then asks three further questions:

- Do you believe and trust in God the Father, who made the world?
- Do you believe and trust in his Son Jesus Christ, who redeemed mankind?
- Do you believe and trust in his Holy Spirit, who gives life to the people of God?

Those being confirmed declare their commitment to the Christian faith in answering these questions. They kneel before the bishop. He places his hands on the head of each one (**B**) and says:

> *'Confirm, O Lord, Your servant* (name) *with Your Holy Spirit.'*

Each one replies 'Amen'. In the Roman Catholic tradition the bishop anoints them with oil (**C**).

After all the candidates have been confirmed the bishop may give a short sermon reminding them of the meaning of their promises and new commitments. In some Churches confirmation is followed by a celebration of Holy Communion. For Anglicans this will be the first time they receive the bread and the wine.

### THINGS TO DO

1 Design a poster advertising the fact that classes are beginning for those wanting to be confirmed. Indicate the reasons someone might have for thinking about taking this step and use questions to catch the attention of the reader.

2 Write an article for a church magazine for young people in which someone describes their confirmation and what it meant for them.

3 There are some things in life which we need to confirm or 'say again' – our commitments, our beliefs, our intentions, our love for someone. Making firm these things can be important. Write a short play or a story which illustrates this idea of 'making firm'.

4 Christians getting confirmed are taking responsibility for their own religious life. What aspects of your life are you now taking responsibility for which others took responsibility for in the past? Write your answer in the form of a letter to a friend who has just told you about their confirmation.

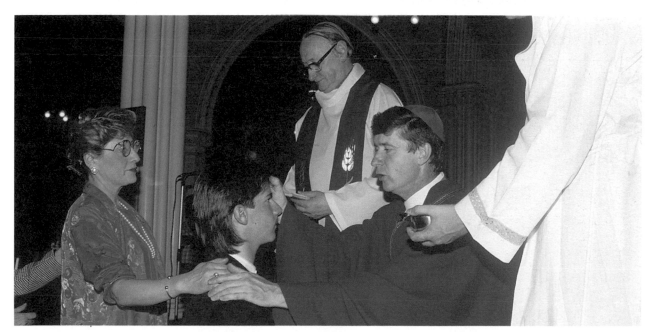

**C** *In the Roman Catholic Church the bishop confirms the candidate*

# Believer's Baptism

In some Churches, for example the Baptist Church, there is no infant baptism or christening service. This is because these Christians believe it is better to wait until the person is old enough to take responsibility for their own faith. To mark this they have a service called **Believer's Baptism**. It is an important step in the Christian's life and expresses his or her readiness to make a full personal commitment to the faith.

In the Bible, Jesus Christ commanded his disciples to baptize believers. Members of the Baptist tradition believe that they are following this commandment. Jesus himself was baptized in the River Jordan. As a reminder of this some Baptists today are baptized in the waters of the sea or a river (**A**). In the UK, most baptisms take place in church.

## Discussion question

*What do you think are the advantages and disadvantages of baptism in a) the sea or a river; b) a church?*

Believers who feel ready to be baptized attend classes which are usually run by the church minister. This is an opportunity to learn about the meaning of baptism and the responsibilities that come with being a committed member of the faith.

In a Baptist church there is a pool called the **baptistry**. It is kept empty and covered up when not in use. The baptism service is usually held during the regular Sunday service. The baptistry is filled with water beforehand. The minister leads the service.

**A** *Some Christians are baptized in the sea or in the waters of a river*

**B** *The believer is lowered into the water*

During the worship, those being baptized stand to make a public declaration of their faith. One at a time they step down into the baptistry. When they are in the water the minister asks the believer:

> *'Do you confess Jesus Christ as your Saviour and Lord?'*

The believer says 'I do'. The minister then says:

> *'On your confession of faith in Jesus Christ as Saviour and Lord, I baptize you in the name of the Father, the Son and the Holy Spirit.'*

Then he supports the believer, lowers them backwards under the water for a brief moment and lifts them up again (**B**). Afterwards hymns are sung and those who have been baptized go to change into dry clothes.

Believer's Baptism requires total immersion under the water. This is symbolic of dying and rising again with Christ. It means leaving behind a life centred on selfishness and starting a life centred on serving Christ. Some followers believe that the water of baptism also represents the washing away of sin.

## THINGS TO DO

1 Imagine you have been present at the baptism of a Baptist friend. Write an account of what happened. Include your thoughts on the meaning of the service.
2 Prepare an illustrated information sheet on Believers' Baptism that could be handed out to new members of a church congregation.
3 With a partner, discuss what might be the different responses to the issue of infant baptism versus Believer's Baptism. Write up a balanced account of the debate which looks at both sides of the argument.
4 Christians believe that the new commitment expressed in baptism should lead to a new life which is no longer self-centred or driven by greed, anger, bitterness or hatred but by love. What sort of life would you regard as a 'new life' from the one you live now? Write a song or poem that explores the idea of your life taking a new direction.

# Marriage

According to the teachings of Christianity, marriage is the union of two people in a faithful relationship of love and companionship for life. Marriage is also intended as an opportunity for sharing in God's creative activity by raising a family. Christians believe that in the marriage ceremony God is involved in the joining of the two lives. Marriage ceremonies may vary from one Christian Church to another but they express these same beliefs (**A**).

Before agreeing to marry a couple in church, the minister or priest will arrange to meet the bride and groom. This is to make sure the couple understands the meaning of Christian marriage and gives them the opportunity to think about the vows that they will be making.

**B** *The bride and groom exchange wedding vows before an Anglican minister*

**A** *A couple being married in an Orthodox church*

At the wedding ceremony in the Anglican Church the bride and groom stand facing the minister at the altar (**B**). To begin the service he reminds everyone present that:

*'We have come together in the presence of God, to witness the marriage of (name) and (name) and to ask His blessing on them. The scriptures teach us that marriage is a gift of God in creation and a means of His grace, a holy mystery in which man and woman become one flesh.'*

The minister leads the marriage service. It includes hymns, prayers, readings from the Bible and there is often a sermon. The minister asks if anyone knows of any lawful reason why the couple should not be joined in marriage. He names the groom and asks:

*'Will you take (name) to be your wife? Will you love her, comfort her, honour and protect her and, forsaking all others, be faithful to her as long as you both shall live?'*

The groom answers and the bride is then asked the same questions. When both have made their vows they are asked to repeat after the minister:

*'I take you, to be my husband/wife, to have and to hold from this day forward; for better for worse, for richer for poorer, in sickness and in health, to love and to cherish, till death us do part, according to God's holy law; and this is my solemn vow.'*

## Discussion question

*Many couples who are not practising or church-going Christians still want to marry in a church. Should the church provide this service?*

The groom puts the ring on his wife's finger. Sometimes the groom receives a ring from his bride (**C**). The bride and groom are then declared to be man and wife and the minister reminds the congregation:

*'That which God has joined together, let no man divide.'*

## THINGS TO DO

1 Look through this unit again. Write an account of Christian beliefs regarding marriage. Say whether you agree or disagree with them.
2 Write a script for the Christian marriage service which could be used over a video film of the wedding. Give details of the vows that are made and other significant points such as the symbols used and words of prayers and promises.
3 Promising to love, comfort, protect and be faithful – these are some of the essential features of the Christian marriage ceremony. How could these be represented in symbols? Design a marriage banner that could be hung in churches during weddings.
4 Design your own marriage ceremony. Be clear about the vows that you think the couple should make. Write out the words for the service and include ideas for symbols, readings, poems or prayers, music and any other special arrangements.

**C** *The exchange of rings is a symbol of unity*

# 30 Death

Christians believe that Christ rose from the dead. This is called the **Resurrection**. They believe this was a sign that Christ had overcome the power of death. In the Gospels there are accounts of the **disciples** going to the tomb where Jesus was buried and finding it empty, and also of the disciples meeting the risen Christ. The resurrection of Christ is the basis for what St Paul says about the day of resurrection at the end of time:

> *'We shall not all die, but when the last trumpet sounds, we shall all be changed in an instant, as quickly as the blinking of an eye. For when the trumpet sounds, the dead will be raised, never to die again and we shall all be changed. For what is mortal must be changed into what is immortal.'*

(I Corinthians 15:51–53)

**A** *Roman Catholics believe that after death the soul will go to Heaven, Hell or Purgatory according to the life that has been led*

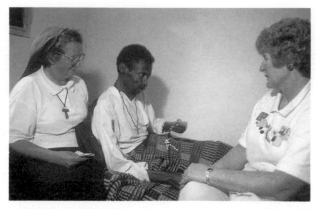

**B** *Christians believe they should visit the sick and dying*

Christians believe that we cannot know exactly what happens after death. Some say that the physical body dies but that at the resurrection we will be raised in a spiritual body. Many Christians believe that when the body dies the soul survives and is reunited with God.

The Roman Catholic faith teaches its followers that after death the souls of the good and pure go to **Heaven** (**A**). However, the majority are not so saintly. Those who have lived evil lives and who have rejected the love of God go to be punished in **Hell**. Those who have sinned but who repent and accept God's forgiveness spend time in **Purgatory**. This is to pay for their wrong-doings and prepare them for Heaven.

### Discussion question

*What do you think would be the difference between a physical body and a spiritual body?*

One of the most important tasks that Christian ministers and priests are involved in is helping the sick and the dying to prepare for death. They may visit the person who is very ill and spend time in prayer with them (**B**). They may take the bread and wine to celebrate Holy Communion with them in their home or at the hospice or hospital. The minister or priest may need to listen to their concerns or anxieties or offer comfort by just sitting quietly with them.

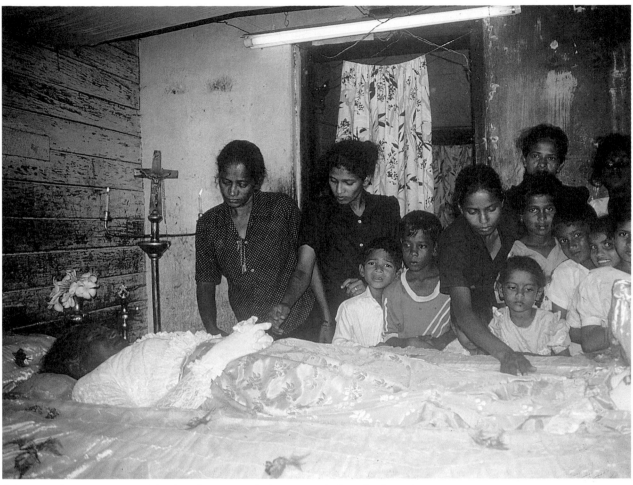

**C** *In some Christian communities loved ones pay their respects before the funeral*

When a person dies the body is washed and dressed and laid in a coffin. It may be kept in the chapel at the funeral parlour or taken to the home of the bereaved where prayers are said. In the Orthodox and Roman Catholic traditions, the coffin is sometimes left open at the chapel until the end of the funeral service so that friends can come and pay respects and pray for the soul of the person who has died (**C**).

## THINGS TO DO

1 Using the words of St Paul and the text concerning the Christian beliefs about life after death, prepare questions to ask people about their beliefs. Find out which beliefs are the most popular. Write up your conclusions.

2 Write a summary of the ways in which priests and church ministers offer their time, help and support, and their services to those who are dying.

3 In the quotation from the Bible in this Unit, St Paul has a very positive message for Christians concerned about death. There are both positive images and negative images in the way people express their beliefs about death. Design a collage or poster which explores both aspects of these approaches to death.

4 Christians are reminded of the death of Christ when they look at the cross. What might make someone really stop and think about death and what it means? Discuss this question in writing. Say whether you believe that people should think more carefully about death and what it means.

## 31

# The funeral

The Christian Church allows burial or **cremation**. The family follows the wishes of the person who has died in this matter. The minister or priest from the church to which the deceased belonged meets with close members of the family to make arrangements for the funeral service. The person who has died may have chosen hymns and prayers and left other instructions for their funeral. If not, the family will choose them or accept the guidance of the minister.

### Discussion question

*Some Christians leave very clear instructions about what kind of funeral they would like to have. Do you think this is a good idea? Why is this helpful?*

The funeral service may take place at the crematorium (**A**) or the church. Prayers are said giving thanks for the person's life and commending their soul to God. The minister gives a short sermon offering words of comfort to the bereaved, reminding them of the life and contribution of the one who has died. Close friends or relatives may say a few words paying tribute to the life of the departed. Sometimes they are involved in reading or reciting poetry or they might lead the prayers.

If the body is to be buried, the mourners go to the graveside. The priest or minister recites words from the scriptures reminding them of the promise of the resurrection (see Unit 30). As it is lowered into the ground, the minister scatters soil on the top of the coffin (**B**) saying:

*'We commit* (name's) *body to the ground, earth to earth, ashes to ashes, dust to dust.'*

**A** *The funeral service may take place at a crematorium rather than in a church*

**B** *As the coffin is lowered into the ground, the minister scatters soil on to it*

She or he then says a few words of blessing to end the service. Friends and relatives leave flowers and wreaths.

Usually the family gathers after the funeral for something to eat and drink. This is also a time to offer comfort to those who were very close to the one who has died. In some Christian communities, the gathering of friends and family after the funeral becomes a celebration and thanksgiving for the life of the one who has passed away.

When the body is cremated the ashes are collected later and usually scattered in the garden of rest at the crematorium. Sometimes the person who has died leaves instructions about where the ashes should be taken for scattering.

The funeral service varies slightly from one tradition to another. For example, in the Roman Catholic Church there is a celebration of Mass at the start of the funeral. However, in all the Christian traditions one message is the same – that the promise of God's love is stronger than death itself.

### THINGS TO DO

1 Give an account of a Christian burial or cremation service in words and pictures which could be used to explain what was happening to children present at the service.

2 Write a script for an interview in which a Christian priest or minister is asked to describe what they do at either the cremation or the burial service.

3 What are the things that are important in a Christian funeral service? Should it be a celebration, a service of thanksgiving or should it be a totally sad and serious occasion? Write an article for a magazine in which you discuss these questions and describe the kind of occasion you think is appropriate.

4 'Life must go on.' Is life stronger than death? What evidence is there that death does not have the last say? How can people make sure that death and the fear of it does not rule their lives? Write a poem or prayer or song which celebrates the fact that life is stronger than death.

# 32

# Islam: freedom to choose

Muslims believe that **Allah** is the giver of all life – not only the life we have now but also life after death. This is explained in the teachings of the Muslim holy book, the **Qur'an (A)**:

> 'Surely He makes the dead alive and surely He has the power to do everything; there is no doubt that the hour will come and truly Allah will raise those who are in graves'
>
> (22:5–7)

With this gift of life from Allah comes the freedom to choose how to live. On the one hand a person can follow their own desires and live a self-centred existence. Or they can follow the will of Allah and live a God-centred life. Islam means submission and Muslims are men and women who submit to the will of Allah.

**A** *Muslims live by the teachings of the Qur'an*

**B** *The world of work is not separate from the world of faith in Islam*

### Discussion question

When we are given a choice about something it means we are also being given responsibility. What examples can you give to show these two go together?

In the **Hadith**, which contains the words of the Prophet **Muhammad**, he is reported as saying:

> 'Every new born child is by nature a Muslim. It is his parents who make a Jew, a Christian or a Zoroastrian of him.'

In other words, children are born with a natural inclination to trust and obey. These are essential qualities of the true Muslim.

There is no special ceremony by which a person becomes a Muslim. Someone who obeys the will of Allah is a Muslim and this submission is expressed in a simple declaration of belief and in the way the person lives. Muslims declare their faith by the words:

*'There is no God but Allah and Muhammad is Allah's Messenger.'*

This statement of faith is the **Shahadah**, the first of the **Five Pillars of Islam**. These are the duties a Muslim must fulfil.

The life of the Muslim is shaped by the Five Pillars. **Salah**, the second pillar, is prayer said five times a day. So the Muslim day is structured around worship. Islam does not separate life into religious and non-religious activities. The world of work and earning a living is not separate from the world of faith (**B**). **Zakah**, the third pillar, is giving to the poor. Every Muslim must give two-and-a-half per cent of their savings to those in need. To observe **Ramadan**, the month of fasting, is the fourth pillar of Islam. Every year Muslims are required to put the will of Allah before their own physical needs and desires for one month. The fifth pillar is **Hajj**, the pilgrimage to **Makkah**, the birthplace of the Prophet Muhammed, which every Muslim must try to make at least once in their lifetime.

In these ways the day, the year and the life of the Muslim are each given shape and meaning by acts of submission and devotion to Allah.

### THINGS TO DO

1 Explain in writing how the day, the year and the life of the Muslim are all shaped by the Five Pillars of Islam.
2 Write a script in which a TV or radio interviewer asks a Muslim and a non-believer about free will and the choices we are given in life. Try to show a difference between the Muslim approach to life and the attitude of a non-believer.
3 The day of the Muslim is structured around prayer. How is your day, year, life structured – by the school timetable, by television programmes, by special days, by visits to relatives and friends (**C**)? Describe the structures that surround your life. Say how you would feel if these were taken away.
4 Muslims say we are responsible for our choices in life and when we die we will be answerable to Allah for the choices we have made. Write a short story in which a person comes to realize for the first time that they are responsible for the way they live.

**C** *How is your day structured?*

# 33

# Birth and naming

Muslims believe that the gift of life is very precious. The birth of a baby is therefore an occasion of great joy and thanksgiving. Muslim parents feel that it is both a great responsibility and a great privilege to be able to bring children into the world and to raise them in the Muslim faith.

Soon after the birth of a child, the father or another member of the family repeats the **Adhan** in the baby's right ear (**A**). This is the Muslim call to prayer, which, in Muslim countries, the **mu'adhin** declares five times a day from the top of the **minaret** at the **mosque** (**B**). It begins with the words: 'God is greatest' or 'Allahu Akbar'. This is repeated four times. Then the **Iqamah**, which is a call to the faithful, is whispered into the left ear of the baby. It ends with the words 'There is no God but Allah'. This

**B** The call to prayer is heard five times a day

simple ritual is the first step in the nurture of the child in the Muslim faith. It is not seen as an initiation because a person can only be a Muslim of their own free will.

## Discussion question

*If a person is brought up with no faith and no religious tradition, can they have a real choice about whether they want to be religious or not? Explain your thoughts on this.*

Several days after the birth there is a ceremony held at home. This is called the **aqiqah**. The baby's head is shaved of its fine hair as a symbol of purification (**C**). Traditionally, on this occasion parents give the weight of the hair in silver to charity. The aqiqah is marked by an act of sacrifice. In the case of a boy, two sheep are bought

**A** The Adhan is whispered in the baby's right ear

and killed and one if it is a girl. The meat is prepared by the **halal** butcher and divided into three portions. One is kept for the family. Another is for the friends and relatives and is usually prepared as a meal to have after the ceremony. The third portion is given to the poor and needy. In this way the family share their good fortune and happiness with others.

The naming of the child takes place on this occasion. For a baby boy it can be taken from the names in the Qur'an and may be that of one of the prophets. It is chosen for its meaning. A girl's name may also be taken from the Qur'an. When the ceremony is over there is a celebration meal.

Muslim boys are circumcised. There is no hard and fast ruling about when this should take place. Most Muslim parents arrange for it to be carried out at the local hospital if there are facilities available. No special religious ceremony is attached to the occasion. However, it is often celebrated with a family gathering and festive meal.

## THINGS TO DO

1 Write an account of the ways in which the Muslim family celebrates the birth of their child. Try to explain the meaning of the activities.
2 Divide a page into two columns. At the top put the two titles: 'In a non-religious home' and 'In a Muslim home'. Underneath write those activities, feelings, celebrations and decisions that mark the birth of a new baby. There will be some things that are the same in both columns.
3 Write a discussion between a religious and a non-religious person giving arguments for and against raising a child in a religious way of life.
4 Muslims believe a child is learning about its faith from the moment it is born. What do you think are the first things a baby learns? What can the baby tell from the way it is held, fed, spoken to, looked at? What does this tell you about the responsibilities of the parents? Write a poem as if from the baby's point of view saying how much it can tell from its experiences in the first months of life.

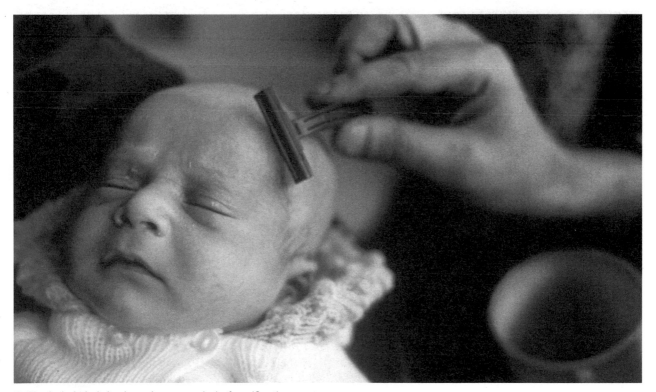

**C** *The baby's hair is shaved as a symbol of purification*

# 34

# Growing up in Islam

There is no special ritual to celebrate the commitment and responsibilities of the believer in Islam. There is no initiation ceremony for entering the faith and no rite of passage which marks the beginning of adult life. Muslim children attend classes at the mosque to learn to read Arabic and to recite the Qur'an. The mosque school is called **madrasah** (**A**). Young Muslims learn about their faith and begin to take on more responsibility for their own religion as they grow up, but that does not make them any more Muslim than they were before.

Education is regarded as very important in Islam and young people are encouraged to devote much time to study (**B**). Every young person learns to recite the Qur'an. Some make a decision to become **hafiz**, that

**B** Education is regarded as very important to Muslims

is someone who can recite the entire Qur'an from memory (**C**). However, there is no requirement for this. It is a matter of individual choice.

Most Muslim parents would like girls and boys to have separate classes when they reach secondary school; in this way they can follow the teachings of the Qur'an. There are guidelines in the Muslim holy book which require women to avoid a situation where they are in male company without a member of the family present. It is also believed that separate classes make it easier for young people to concentrate on their studies without distractions. Many Muslim parents want their children to attend Muslim schools so that the teaching of the faith can play a central role in their education. So far there is no provision for separate Muslim state schools in the UK.

**A** Muslim children attending the mosque school, which is called madrasah

## Discussion question

*In the UK there are Roman Catholic and Church of England schools in the state system. Do you think it is time there were schools with a Muslim foundation? Give reasons for your view.*

As they grow up, young Muslims are encouraged to become more personally responsible for following the teachings of the Qur'an. For example, men and women are required to dress modestly. For women this means wearing clothes that cover the body except for the face and hands. Reaching an age when they can take on the requirements of fasting during the month of Ramadan is another important step in the life of the young Muslim. They may begin with a few days fasting at first. Gradually they will be able to build up to fasting for the full month. When a Muslim keeps the full fast for the first time there is a great sense of achievement. It shows that the young person has learnt the important lesson of self-discipline and has demonstrated a commitment to following the path of Islam.

## THINGS TO DO

1 Describe in writing three ways in which a young person being brought up in the Muslim faith may demonstrate a growing commitment to Islam.

2 Imagine your best friend is a Muslim and has made the decision to try to become hafiz or has decided to complete the full month of fasting. Write the script for a conversation in which you talk together about the different things you are striving for as you grow up and what they mean to you.

3 Research shows that girls do better in single-sex schools. Is this a good enough reason for keeping schools separate for girls and boys? What other arguments could be brought to bear from a Muslim standpoint? Write up the discussion on this issue in a balanced argument giving different points of view.

4 It is hard for Muslims growing up in a culture where the majority are not religious. It would be easier to follow the path of Islam if everyone else was doing the same. Write a script for a play in which a young Muslim talks about some of these issues.

**C** *Some young Muslims decide to become hafiz, reciting the Qur'an by memory*

# 35 Preparing for marriage

According to the teachings of the Qur'an, men and women were created to be partners in life. Marriage is intended to bring tranquillity, love and protection for both partners. The Prophet Muhammad told his followers that marriage is a religious duty:

> 'When a worshipper of God has taken a wife he has perfected half of his religion. So let him fear God in the other half.'
>
> (Hadith)

Muslim parents believe it is their duty to seek out a suitable marriage partner for their son or daughter. Marriage is regarded as so important that finding the right partner cannot be left to chance meetings (**A**). For this reason, young Muslims are often discouraged from becoming too friendly with members of the opposite sex until they are ready to think about marriage. Sexual relationships outside marriage are strictly forbidden under Islamic law.

**B** *The interests and education of the young person are taken into account when choosing a marriage partner*

Because Muslim parents are involved in choosing a marriage partner for their children, the approach has been described as 'arranged marriage'. However, Muslims prefer the term 'assisted marriage'. Although the parents may introduce their son or daughter to a suitable partner, the young person has a right to say no to the match if they are not happy with the parents' choice. Marriage is arranged only after consultation with the young people involved. Muhammad said:

> 'A girl is to be asked whether she consents to marriage. If she is silent, it counts as assent. If she refuses she is not to be compelled.'
>
> (Hadith)

**A** *Finding the right partner is too important to be left to chance meetings at discos and clubs*

## Discussion question

*What do you think that Muslim parents look for in choosing a partner for their son or daughter?*

On the whole, young Muslims trust their parents to find someone who will make a good husband or wife. They look for someone with a similar commitment to Islam and they will take account of the character and interests of their son or daughter (**B**). Often when a couple are introduced the two families know each other beforehand. Meetings between the families are arranged so that the couple can see each other. If they are both interested then a meeting is arranged at the girl's home so that they can talk together. Assisted marriage is not necessarily without romance. It is true, however, that love usually comes after the couple are married rather than before.

The Qur'an encourages Muslims to marry and have children. Happy family life is considered the basis of a happy society. A marriage is therefore an important occasion for the whole community and not just the individuals concerned. Islamic law allows a man to have up to four wives. However, the husband must be fair to all his wives and treat them equally. Today most Muslim men have only one wife (**C**).

**C** *Most Muslim men now have only one wife*

### THINGS TO DO

1 Write an article for a Muslim newsletter which explains the teachings of the Qur'an and the words of Muhammad in the Hadith on marriage.

2 Prepare a radio or TV programme on assisted marriage in which a Muslim family is in the process of introducing their son or daughter to a suitable partner. Include interviews with different members of the two families involved and show what each is looking for.

3 There are advantages and disadvantages in any system of finding the right marriage partner. Draw up the advantages and disadvantages in the 'leave it to chance' approach and then for the 'parent assisted' approach. Try to give a balanced argument for each case.

4 Design a diagram illustrating the Muslim belief that happy family life is important for the well-being of the whole community.

# 36

# A Muslim wedding

In Islam, marriage is not a union made by God but a human contract. However, it is an agreement made before God and therefore has deep religious significance. Because the parents are involved in making the match (see unit 35), they share some responsibility for making sure the marriage works. This makes it an important occasion for the families as well as the couple themselves. Once they agree to marry, the day for the wedding is set. The two families decide on a dowry, which is a gift of money to the wife on marriage. This is called **mahr**. It is given by the groom and will remain the bride's own property. Some of the mahr may be paid before the marriage, the rest may be held back. This delayed part of the dowry will be paid if the husband divorces his wife. In this way the wife has added security in marriage.

The marriage ceremony is sometimes held at the bride's family home or in a room at the local mosque (**A**). Friends and family are invited. The **imam** usually conducts the service although this can be done by any Muslim male adult. The groom, his father and

**B** Marriage customs may vary from one community to another

the other male friends and relatives gather in a room where the imam begins by asking the groom if he consents to the marriage. Once he has consented the groom then makes his marriage vows in the presence of the imam and witnesses. The bride does not have to be present for this. Her father can represent her. She may wait in a separate room with the female members of the family where witnesses report to her when the groom has made his solemn promise:

*'I (name) take (name) as my lawfully wedded wife before Allah and in the presence of these witnesses, in accordance with the teachings of the holy Qur'an.'*

## Discussion question

*Why do you think that it is important to have a witness at a wedding?*

Allah is called on as the supreme witness to this vow. The groom also promises to make the marriage an act of submission to Allah, and a relationship of love, mercy and peace. The imam recites verses from the Qur'an and prayers for the welfare and happiness of the couple. Once the bride hears that the groom has made his promises she makes her vows too, also in front of the imam and witnesses. The bride and groom then sign copies of the marriage contract and keep one each.

**A** A Muslim bride and groom on their wedding day

At many Muslim wedding ceremonies there are non-religious traditions and customs which follow the formal ceremony. These vary from one community to another (**B**). However, one tradition in common is the celebration meal before the couple set out on their life together (**C**).

## THINGS TO DO

1  Write a programme giving the order of events for the Muslim marriage ceremony to accompany an invitation to friends and relatives.

2  Imagine a discussion between a Muslim who has just married and a non-Muslim who has also recently been wed. Write up a conversation in which they compare their two wedding ceremonies and discuss the similarities and differences.

3  The dowry in Muslim marriage is intended to provide financial security for the wife. What are the things – apart from financial security – that help a person feel secure in marriage? Write advice for a magazine column which encourages newly-weds to give their partner a sense of security and suggest how they might achieve this.

4  Young Muslims have the teachings of their faith and the guidance of parents to help them make decisions about marriage. What are the influences in the lives of young people coming from non-religious backgrounds when it comes to making decisions about love and marriage? Do young people receive the guidance and help that they need for such an important decision in life? Discuss these questions in class and write up your own answer in an essay.

**C** *The celebration meal after the wedding is traditional in most communities*

# 37

# Life after death

Every day the Muslim says this prayer from the Qur'an (**A**):

*'All praise is for Allah, the Lord of the Universe, the most merciful, the most kind; Master of the Day of Judgement. You alone we worship, from You alone we seek help. Guide us along the straight path – the path of those whom You favoured, not of those who earned Your anger or went astray.'*

(Qur'an 1:1–7)

Every day Muslims remember that there is a life to come after death and what they do in this life will decide what happens to them when they die.

However, a Muslim should not serve Allah just for the sake of future rewards. A **Sufi** poet from the mystic tradition in Islam wrote:

*'O my Lord, if I worship You from fear of Hell, burn me in Hell, and if I worship You from hope of Paradise, exclude me there, but if I worship You for Your own sake then do not withhold not from me Your Eternal Beauty.'*

## Discussion question

*What is the poet saying in this prayer about a) the nature of God; b) human nature? What is the meaning of his request?*

According to the teachings of the holy Qur'an there will be a final **Day of Judgement** when everyone will be resurrected from the dead. Muslims believe that on this day

**A** *Every day the Muslim prays, 'All praise is for Allah …'*

everyone will be judged according to the life they have led. Those who have followed the will of Allah will go to **Paradise**. Those who have ignored the will of Allah and have gone astray will be punished.

Muslims believe that everyone is responsible for their actions in this life and will have to answer for them after death. According to Muslim tradition, there are two angels watching over us, keeping a record of our deeds and they will be called on to report how we have conducted our lives.

In the Qur'an, Paradise is described as a beautiful garden where rivers flow and where there is no suffering or hunger but shade from the sun, food to eat and perfect peace (**B**). In contrast **Hell** is a place of torment and unbearable heat.

In Islam life after death is called **Akhirah**. It is one of the basic beliefs of the faith. Every time Muslims pray they remember there will

be a Day of Judgement and a life after death. However, they also remember the kindness and mercy of Allah. Muslims believe that Allah forgives those who turn to him and are sorry and try follow the straight path of Islam.

### THINGS TO DO

1 Use the quotation from the Qur'an and the words of the Sufi poet to write an article on Muslim beliefs about what happens after death.
2 Write a dialogue between a Muslim and a non-Muslim who are discussing whether what we do in this life matters.
3 What is your idea of Paradise? Is it to be found here in this world or in the world to come? Write down your own thoughts and ideas on this.
4 To Muslims, Allah is merciful. This is one of his essential qualities. What is mercy? Write a story to illustrate the meaning of the word.

**B** *In the Muslim tradition gardens sometimes represent Paradise, a place of perfect peace*

# 38

# Funeral rites

Muslims believe that this life is a preparation for the life after death. They therefore try to live in a way that is pleasing to Allah, guided by the Five Pillars. The last of these, the Hajj, is regarded by many as an important step in preparation for death (**A**). The peace and sense of community experienced on the pilgrimage to Makkah is a foretaste of the peace of Paradise. Many Muslims believe that the Hajj purifies and cleanses the soul of past evil.

As a Muslim approaches death they will recite the words of the Shahadah. Close relatives or friends will stay with them and read verses from the Qur'an. When death comes the family gathers and recites the following words from the Qur'an:

*'We belong to Allah and to Him we shall return.'*

In Islam the body must be buried as soon as possible after death. Muslims believe that everyone will be raised from the dead. It is for this reason that the body is not destroyed by **cremation** but is shown great care and respect. It is washed three times as if for prayer and then all over with soap and water. It is anointed with perfume and wrapped in three pieces of white cloth. If the deceased has been on the Hajj these cloths will be the ones worn on the pilgrimage. The body is then laid in a coffin, on its left side.

## Discussion question

*Most large, purpose-built mosques have a mortuary. Why do you think this is?*

The coffin is carried to the mosque and is placed so that the body faces Makkah. Family and friends and other members of the local Muslim community gather there. The imam may lead the prayers. The first

**A** *Many Muslims see the Hajj as an important step in the preparation for death*

**B** *The coffin is taken to the cemetery for burial. Cremation is not allowed in Islam*

1 Prepare a set of guidelines to inform social workers on the way Muslims prepare for death and on Muslim burial rites.

2 Which of the Five Pillars is particularly connected to Muslim traditions concerning death? Write out each of the Five Pillars as a heading. Underneath say whether each particular one is significant in relation to death, and what part it plays in Muslim preparation for death and funeral rites.

3 People sometimes have quite strong feelings about whether they are going to be buried or cremated. Others say exactly what they want at their funeral service. What are the concerns and feelings that are behind these preferences? Why do people want death to be marked in a special way? Write your answer as a part of a conversation with someone who has avoided thinking about their funeral.

4 Muslims believe it is important to remember the dead. Remembering is an important part of coming to terms with the loss of a loved one. Write a poem or a prayer or design a card which explores this theme of remembrance.

chapter of the Qur'an is repeated. The coffin is then taken to the cemetery for burial (**B**). As it is lowered into the grave, the following words from the Qur'an are said:

> *'From the earth we did create you and into it we shall return and from it shall we bring you out once again.'*

Muslims believe that it is important to pray for and remember their deceased relatives, especially their parents. In some parts of the world, they keep a special night called the **Night of Forgiveness**. This night is in the middle of the month of Ramadan, the month of fasting. Followers of Islam believe that on this night their life for the coming year is determined by Allah. During the course of the night, they spend time in prayer and many fast the day before. In some Muslim communities, the men visit the graves of loved ones and think about the coming of the Day of Judgement (**C**).

**C** *Some Muslims believe it is important to visit the graves of loved ones who have died*

# 39

# Sikhism: many lives, one journey

According to the Sikh scriptures, the **Guru Granth Sahib**, the soul travels through many lives. After many births in different bodies and different forms it eventually reaches human existence. It is only at this stage in the soul's journey that it can attain **mukti**. This is when the soul is liberated from the endless cycle of death and rebirth and finds union with God.

## Discussion question

*How is the word 'liberation' generally used? What ideas does it carry with it? How is the word being used here in relation to the cycle of death and rebirth?*

According to Sikh belief, this human existence we are in now is therefore to be treasured. It is an opportunity to come to know God and to learn how to be close to him. Sikhs usually call God **Waheguru**, which means 'Wonderful Lord'. They believe that it is God's will that all people should come to know and love him. According to the Sikh scriptures, it is God who awakens the human soul and calls men and women to him. It is by God's grace that the soul attains liberation and union with him.

A person only survives and grows physically if they belong to a caring community which feeds and protects and nurtures them. Similary Sikhs believe that a person only develops spiritually and morally if they belong to a community where spiritual and moral values are nurtured (**A**). The Sikh way of life provides an example of the sort of community in which *all* aspects of human development are cared for. This is called the **Sadhsangat**. The Sadhsangat is an ideal society in miniature where both physical and spiritual needs are met. Humility, tolerance, patience, service, justice, mercy and kindness are encouraged and acted out in practical ways. These qualities are seen as an expression of the knowledge and love of Waheguru.

The **Gurdwara**, the Sikh place of worship, is where the Sikh Sadhsangat is able to serve the wider community. Worship at the Gurdwara provides spiritual nourishment through the reading of the scriptures (**B**), prayer and devotional hymns or **kirtan**. The **langar** provides food for physical nourishment and is an example of the value of sharing (**C**). According to the Sikh scriptures, we must not waste the

**A** *Where do children develop their moral and spiritual values?*

**B** *The reading of the scriptures provides spiritual nourishment*

opportunity in this life to grow spiritually and come to know God. Through the Sadhsangat and the Gurdwara, Sikhism helps its followers to meet this challenge.

**C** *The meal in the langar provides physical nourishment*

## THINGS TO DO

1 Write a summary of Sikh beliefs about the following:
   a the cycle of life, death and rebirth;
   b the relationship between God and human beings;
   c the importance of the relationship between the individual and the community.

2 Draw a diagram to show the physical and the spiritual needs of an individual. You could draw a person in the middle of your page and using words and symbols indicate the different needs, e.g. food, warmth, education, moral guidance, etc. Underneath say which of these needs the Gurdwara meets.

3 Sikhs believe that human life offers the unique opportunity to find union with God. What do you see as the important opportunities in life? Write your answer in the form of a letter to a Sikh friend who has explained his or her beliefs about the opportunity of life.

4 Schools in the UK are required by law to make provision for the 'spiritual development' of pupils. How should a school do this? Which subjects can offer the best opportunity for spiritual development? Make a collection of your ideas in writing and put together a classroom display of your work.

# 40

# All stages in life are one

The first of the Sikh gurus, **Guru Nanak** (**A**), saw that the way to God is open to every human being no matter which religion or class in society they belonged to. He also saw that God must be found in everyday life.

Guru Nanak was concerned about the many restrictions in religion which in effect prevented people from coming close to God. For example, some people believed that to reach union with God you had to give up your livelihood, your home, your family and become a recluse in the forest. They believed that to attain union with God you had to endure great hardship, practising the most difficult forms of **yoga** and meditation and relying on begging for food (**B**). Guru Nanak rejected this idea. He said there was no point in shutting yourself off from the world. God could be found in everyday life. He did not require a person to leave house and home to live in the forest as a hermit.

Others believed that you could only reach liberation in the final stage of life. This meant first completing the stage of being a student and then of being a householder with all the responsibilities of earning a living and raising a family. Only after retirement could a person turn to the quest for liberation and union with God. Guru Nanak also rejected this idea. He taught his followers that the way to mukti is open to everyone, no matter what their age and stage in life.

## Discussion question

*Do you think that there are times in life when people are more likely to look for or turn to God? What times are these? Why do people turn to God then?*

**A** *The first of the Sikh gurus, Guru Nanak*

**B** *Guru Nanak said you did not have to perform difficult yoga positions to come close to God*

According to the teachings of Sikhism, we are all involved in and rely on the world of work. We all have responsibilities as part of a family and we all have a role to play in the community. No one can survive without other people. No one can live without relying on the world of work one way or another (**C**). It is therefore only right to contribute, earn a living by honest means, and to share one's resources.

Guru Nanak said men and women must remember God while they are in the busy world of work and involved in family life. There is no reason to wait until these responsibilities are over. In a community that serves both the physical and spiritual needs of the people there is the opportunity to come to know and love God and to find union with him in the very heart of everyday life.

## THINGS TO DO

1 Draw a diagram to represent the four stages in life. You could draw a circle which is divided up like four pieces of a cake. In each section write about the stage it represents. Finally write a short paragraph on the Sikh attitude towards drawing close to God during the various stages of life.

2 Design a leaflet or poster which shows that, according to Sikhism, the way to God is open to everyone no matter what their age or stage in life.

3 Is it true, as Guru Nanak taught, that we all depend on a society in which people have to work and earn a living? If we depend on this world of work should we contribute towards it? How can we make a contribution to the society we live in if we are not able to find work? Discuss these questions in class. Write up your answer in the form of a newspaper article which includes the different points of view which emerge from your discussion.

4 Finding time for God or just for thinking about life and where it leads is difficult in a busy world. It is something that often gets put to one side. What are the arguments and excuses a person could make for putting off thinking about these things? Write a monologue, a poem, a short play or a prayer in which a person keeps avoiding these really important questions and never gets round to considering them seriously.

**C** *We are all involved in and rely on the world of work*

# 41 The naming ceremony

According to the teachings of Sikhism, this life is a precious gift. Birth is therefore a time for rejoicing and giving thanks to God.

*'Joy abounds in all creation, praise Him you who love your Lord God Almighty. Perfect Master, all pervading, everywhere.*
*God's eternal word has reached us, chasing far our grief and care. God is gracious, filled with mercy, Nanak thus proclaims this truth.'*

(Guru Granth Sahib)

When a new baby is born, prayers of joy and thanksgiving are recited from the Guru Granth Sahib. Sometimes one of the prayers of Guru Nanak is whispered in the ear of the newborn child. In some families, arrangements are made for a reading of the full text of the Guru Granth Sahib to mark the special occasion and to give thanks to God.

Usually the parents take gifts to the Gurdwara as a sign of thanksgiving to God. A family may donate a rumala or silk cloth as a cover for the Guru Granth Sahib. They may also make a donation of money or food. At a later date they may take responsibility for the community meal in the langar after worship at the Gurdwara, as an expression of thanks and a desire to share their happiness with others in the community.

## Discussion question

*Sharing happiness with others is important. Why do we need to share our joys and successes?*

Shortly after the birth there is a naming ceremony. This is usually held during the regular congregational worship at the Gurdwara (**A**). Friends and relatives are

**A** *The joy of the birth is shared with the community at the naming ceremony*

**B** *The granthi reading from the scriptures*

invited. The **granthi** leads the ceremony. He invites the parents to come and sit at the front before the Guru Granth Sahib. Then reverently and carefully he lifts the pages of the holy book and lets them fall open. The first letter for the child's name is taken from the first letter of the first word at the start of the hymn on the top of the left-hand page. The parents choose a name, sometimes with the help of close relatives present. When it has been chosen, the granthi announces it to the congregation and recites a blessing (**B**).

Sometimes the child is given **amrit** at the naming ceremony. This consists of a mixture of sugar and water. It is stirred in a small bowl with a double-edged ritual sword called a **khanda** while prayers are recited over it. The granthi dips the khanda into the amrit and very lightly touches the tongue of the baby. The rest of the mixture is given to the mother to drink.

Sikh first names are important because they are chosen for their meaning. Most Sikh first names can be for either sex. Guru Gobind Singh wanted all Sikhs to be treated as equal. He said that the second name should be **Kaur** meaning 'Princess' for a girl or **Singh** meaning 'Lion' for a boy.

## THINGS TO DO

1 Write a newspaper article for your local newspaper explaining what happens at the Sikh naming ceremony. Make sure the article is written in such a way that it helps the reader to understand the importance of the occasion.

2 Design a card for a Sikh naming ceremony inviting friends and relatives to join the family in choosing a name for their new baby at the Gurdwara and encouraging them to stay for langar after the ceremony.

3 Sikhs share their joy of having a child by sharing their wealth in paying for the langar at the Gurdwara. There is no fun in having joy and good news but no one to share it with. Write a play or a story which shows how happiness grows when it is shared.

4 Names are important for their meaning in Sikhism. For example, Gurbakhsh Singh means 'Blessed by the Guru'. It is hoped that the life or character of the child will be shaped by a good name. What is the meaning of your name? Which would you choose for your own children? Choose six names – male and female – and explain in writing why you have chosen them.

# Taking Amrit

As they approach adulthood, many young Sikhs take part in ceremony somtimes called **Amrit chhakna**. This is an initiation ceremony in which they are made members of the **Khalsa**, the community of committed Sikhs.

The ceremony was introduced by the Tenth Guru, Guru Gobind Singh, at the festival of **Baisakhi** in 1699. On this occasion he initiated five men who were willing to give up their lives for the Sikh faith. He called them the **Panj Piare**, the Five Pure Ones (**A**). They became the first members of the Khalsa.

**A** *Guru Gobind Singh with the Panj Piare*

### Discussion question

*Why do you think that Guru Gobind Singh called the volunteers the Five Pure Ones?*

Today the Amrit ceremony is held at the Gurdwara. Those taking Amrit bathe, wash their hair and put on clean clothes. Five members of the Khalsa, called the Panj Piare, perform the ceremony. Those taking Amrit stand before them. They promise to follow the teachings of the Gurus and to obey the following rules for living:

- To pray daily: every morning before dawn and after sunset and before going to bed.
- To wear the **Five Ks**, the symbols of the Sikh faith which all begin with the letter K: **kesh**, long hair; **kangha**, comb; **kara** bracelet; **kachera**, shorts; and **kirpan**, sword.
- To refrain from all intoxicating drinks and drugs.
- To be faithful in marriage.

At the beginning of the ceremony hymns from the Guru Granth Sahib are recited. The Panj Piare prepare a bowl of amrit or nectar and stir the mixture with the **khanda** (**B**). Prayers from the words of the Gurus are said over it. Those who are taking Amrit kneel before the Panj Piare. The nectar is given five times into their cupped hands. It is sprinkled over their eyes and on their head five times. This represents their intention to refrain from evil and to grow in faith. They declare:

*'The Khalsa is dedicated to God. The victory belongs to God alone.'*

All who receive Amrit drink the remaining nectar from the bowl. Finally they recite the **Mool Mantar** five times as a declaration of their belief in God.

**B** *Preparing Amrit*

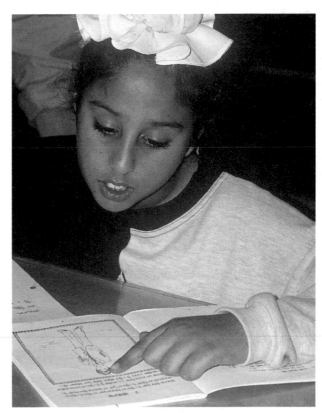

**C** *A young Sikh learning about the teachings of his faith*

After this ceremony, boys receive the second name Singh and girls Kaur. These replace the family names. This is to help break down the barriers between people as traditionally the names used to indicate caste or social position. At the end of the ceremony, a prayer called the **Ardas** is recited. Everyone then receives **karah parshad** (blessed food).

Sikhs can become members of the Khalsa at any age as long as they are old enough to understand the promises and commitments they are making (**C**). Many take Amrit just as they approach adulthood. It is a time when a young person is expected to take a personal responsibility for their beliefs and actions.

### THINGS TO DO

1 Prepare a talk on what it means to become a member of the Sikh Khalsa. Explain how a young Sikh would regard the Amrit ceremony as an important step in life.

2 Prepare an invitation to the Amrit ceremony which has a brief description of what happens so that those who are not Sikh know what to expect. Use some of the Sikh symbols to illustrate your work.

3 The Amrit ceremony is a time for Sikhs to make serious promises for life. What promises have you made about the way you live your life? Invent and describe a ceremony to mark the beginning of adulthood for young people who are not religious. Say what promises should be made and what rules for living they should keep to.

4 Identity and a sense of belonging are important to many young Sikhs. How do young people who are not religious express their sense of identity and belonging today? Write an article for a magazine discussing the way in which young people from different backgrounds do this.

# 43 Marriage

Sikhs believe that marriage is the union of two people in body, mind and soul. It is a relationship for life built on respect, love, equality, humility and faithfulness (**A**).

Sikh parents consider it their duty to find a suitable marriage partner for their son or daughter. However, the young person is involved in the decision and does not have to accept their parents' choice. In the case of disagreement, the proposal is dropped and the search for another partner begins. It is usual among Sikhs to have a betrothal ceremony once a decision has been made.

The Sikh wedding is called **anand karaj**, which means the 'ceremony of bliss'. It must take place in the presence of the Guru Granth Sahib, so most marriages are held at the Gurdwara (**B**). The bride's family acts as host. As the groom's family arrives the two parties greet each other and exchange gifts.

The religious service begins with the musicians singing hymns. The bride and groom sit facing the Guru Granth Sahib. The granthi is usually called upon to conduct the ceremony. He reminds the couple of their commitments and responsibilities in marriage and stresses the importance of faithfulness, kindness and humility in the relationship.

The couple is asked whether it is their wish to be married. They show their acceptance by bowing before the Guru Granth Sahib. The bride's father then takes one end of the scarf worn by the groom and puts it into the hand of his daughter. The marriage hymn from the Guru Granth Sahib is recited. This is the **Lavan**. It is a hymn of praise to God which celebrates the love of the marriage relationship. The love and closeness between the husband and wife is seen as a model for the closeness that can be found between the soul and God.

The couple then walk four times in a complete circle around the Guru Granth Sahib. The first time round is for a life of sharing, work and action. The second is for the coming together of the bride and groom in a relationship of love without fear. The third time around is for detachment from the world of possessions, desires and self-pride. The last time is for the peace of perfect union.

**A** *Sikh marriage is based on respect, humility and equality*

**B** *Most Sikh marriages are held at the Gurdwara*

### Discussion question

*Why do you think the couple walk around the Guru Granth Sahib? What do you think this symbolic action represents?*

The couple is declared husband and wife and they are showered with flower petals. The granthi opens the Guru Granth Sahib once more. This time he reverently and carefully lets the pages fall open and reads the hymn from the left-hand page. This is the final prayer before the end of the service when everyone receives karah parshad. The ceremony is followed by a festive meal and celebration.

### THINGS TO DO

1 Imagine you have been invited to the marriage of a Sikh friend. Write an account of what happened for someone who was not able to go to the wedding.

2 Describe in writing the symbols and symbolic actions in the Sikh wedding ceremony and explain the religious significance of the occasion. Illustrate your work to draw attention to some of the essential features of the ceremony.

3 Sikhs believe that marriage helps people to grow closer to God. In what ways can marriage be a time to develop and grow? What happens if people do not learn and grow in the course of their marriage? Do people think carefully about this aspect when they make their vows? Discuss these questions in class and then write up an account of the answers and include your own thoughts on the matter.

4 According to Sikh teachings, marriage should be a relationship of 'love without fear'. What are the fears that might destroy a marriage? How can a couple ensure that fear does not creep into the relationship? Write a prayer or a poem or a reading called 'Love without fear' that could be said at a wedding ceremony.

# 44 Death and cremation

Sikhs believe that it is possible to find liberation in this life. By following the teachings of the Gurus and meditating on the name of God, a Sikh can become God-filled and reach mukti (see Unit 39). If a person reaches mukti, when they die they are united with God. However, if the soul does not attain mukti it will be born again in another body and continue its journey in another life.

When a Sikh dies the family joins together in the words of prayers from the Guru Granth Sahib. The body is washed with a mixture made from water and yoghurt and clean clothes are put on it. If the person was a Khalsa Sikh, the body is dressed in the Five Ks.

Sikhs cremate their dead. In this way the body is reduced to dust and ashes and rejoins the elements. In India, the body is laid on a funeral pyre in the open air. In the UK, the body is laid in a coffin and **cremation** takes place at the local crematorium (**A**). In some communities, the coffin is taken to the Gurdwara and placed before the Guru Granth Sahib where friends and relatives can pay their respects (**B**). Sometimes the coffin rests at the home of the family or at the chapel at the crematorium until the funeral takes place.

On the day of the cremation, prayers are said for the soul of the deceased. The coffin is taken to the crematorium. Close family members and friends follow. There the granthi recites the **Kirtan Sohila** – the evening prayer – which is often sung at funeral services:

> *'Know the real purpose of being here and gather up your treasure under the guidance of the true Guru. Make your mind God's home. If he abides with you undisturbed, you will not be reborn.'*

The coffin is then removed for cremation.

## Discussion question

*Sometimes Sikhs have to use a chapel with Christian symbols as a place to rest the coffin before the cremation takes place. What arrangements could be made at crematoriums to accommodate mourners from different faiths?*

**A** In the UK, cremation takes place at a crematorium

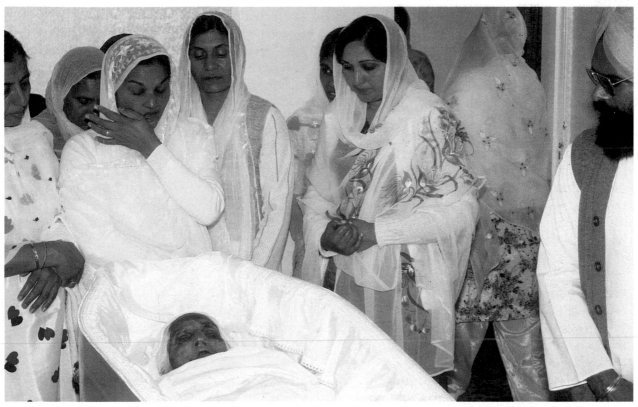

**B** *The coffin may be taken to the Gurdwara where people may pay their respects*

Often there is a service at the Gurdwara following the cremation. Sometimes friends want to say a few words about the person who has died to show their love and respect. The service ends with the usual formal prayer, the Ardas, which is said at most services. Afterwards karah parshad is shared out to the mourners.

After a few days the ashes of the deceased are collected from the crematorium. They are usually taken to a river where they are scattered on the water. The family arranges to have a complete reading of the Guru Granth Sahib after the death of a loved one. Sometimes this takes place at the home but more often it is at the Gurdwara. Towards the end of the reading, friends and relatives gather to remember the deceased and to comfort the family.

## THINGS TO DO

1 Write an account of the Sikh funeral rites as notes for a non-Sikh who is going to attend a funeral and does not know what to expect.
2 Sikhs believe that the soul is on a journey through many lives – at death the soul finds union with God or returns to live again on earth. Represent these different outcomes in the form of a diagram or picture. Explain your diagrams in writing.
3 'Know the real purpose of being here.' These are strong words to which every Sikh is called to respond. Write your own response to this command – what *is* the real purpose of being here? You could write your answer in the form of a diary entry, or just as an account of your own thoughts.
4 The title of Kirtan Sohila – evening prayer – suggests that death is only the night before the new day. Design a card with this theme in mind, which could be sent with words of comfort to a bereaved family. Write your own evening prayer or poem to go inside.

# Shared concerns

The student of religion cannot agree with someone who says that all religions are the same. They are not. Each religious tradition has its own distinctive set of beliefs and practices. If we are to represent each faith in a way that is true to its tradition, we must respect the important differences between them.

## Discussion question

*How would you respond to the person who says all religions are really the same? Would you want to correct their view or put it differently?*

Although there are different beliefs and practices, there are, however, important concerns that the world religions share. For example, all of them make us ask the question: 'Where am I going?' Not one of the great world faiths says to its followers, 'You can go your own way. Do your own thing. Forget about anyone else. You can just do what you want and it doesn't really matter. It makes no difference.' According to all the religious traditions it *does* matter how we live our lives. We do need to think about the direction in which we are going.

The religious ceremonies for marking the turning points and milestones of life are opportunities for all who are present on these occasions to think about their own spiritual journey. At an Anglican christening, everyone is asked to make again their promises to love and serve Christ. At a Jewish wedding, in the midst of all the joy, a glass is broken and the congregation is reminded of the serious side of the occasion. At a Sikh funeral everyone is challenged to 'Know the real purpose of being here'.

**A** *Orthodox churches contain icons of the saints from the past*

**B** *Buddhists meditate on the way all things fade and pass away*

The great religious traditions do not allow a person to be a comfortable and passive passenger on their journey through life. There are important decisions to be made. There are responsibilities to be fulfilled. There are skills and talents that must not be wasted. There are others who are travelling with us that need our help – and sometimes we will need theirs.

In the Christian Orthodox tradition the churches are full of **icons** of the **saints** (**A**). Worshippers are reminded that there have been many who have lived before them. The faces from the past point out to the believer that this life will pass away and what now seems important will one day no longer be so. One of the meditations performed by Buddhist monks is to watch the process of decay (**B**). In this way they learn that nothing is permanent. All things pass. The world's great religions challenge men and women, young and old, to look for that which is unchanging and everlasting – and they say this should be their aim in life (**C**).

## THINGS TO DO

1  Choose two rites from different religions to compare and contrast and to draw out common themes and concerns. For example, you could look at the Sikh Amrit ceremony and Believer's Baptism, or compare two wedding ceremonies.
2  Prepare a play or dialogue between people of different faiths in which they discuss their beliefs about life after death.
3  Marking the seasons of life with religious rituals plays an important part in drawing the community together to remember and celebrate shared values and beliefs. Design a poster celebrating the seasons of life and the values that you think are important in the community. If you prefer, write your suggestion for ways in which the seasons of life could be celebrated in a community where there is no religious belief or practice.
4  What have you learnt through the study of the different faiths? Is there any aspect of religion you would like to know more about? Have you reflected on your own beliefs? Write your answers in the form of an article for a school magazine which is discussing the value of different subjects on the curriculum.

**C** *All the major world religions ask their followers to think about their direction in life*

# Glossary

## A

**Adhan** Muslim call to prayer

**Akhirah** everlasting life, life after death

**Allah** Muslim name for God

**Alms** charity, gift of food

**Altar** table in church from where the Eucharist (bread and wine) is given

**Amrit** nectar made from sugar and water

**Amrit chhakna** Sikh initiation ceremony

**Anand karaj** Sikh wedding ceremony, ceremony of bliss

**Anglican** Christian family of Churches which includes the Church of England

**Anicca** 'impermanence', belief that nothing lasts or has lasting reality

**Aqiqah** ritual shaving of baby's head

**Ardas** formal prayer said in the Gurdwara, sometimes called the standing prayer as Sikhs always stand for it

**Asceticism** self discipline often involving fasting, meditation and giving up comforts of life

**Ashram** community based on a religious or spiritual way of life

**Ashrama** a stage of life (of which there are four in the Hindu tradition)

**Atman** soul, self

## B

**Baisakhi** Sikh festival celebrating the beginning of Sikh Khalsa

**Baptism** rite of initiation which involves sprinkling with water or immersion in water

**Baptist** Christian belonging to Baptist Church, a Protestant Church which rejects practice of infant baptism

**Baptistry** pool or area in church used for Believer's Baptism

**Bar Mitzvah** when a Jewish boy becomes a Son of the Commandment at the age of 13, a ceremony to mark a Jewish boy's coming of age

**Bat Mitzvah** when a Jewish girl becomes a Daughter of the Commandment, a ceremony to mark a Jewish girl's coming of age

**Believer's Baptism** ritual immersion in water as a sign of commitment to Christ

**Bhikkhu** ordained Buddhist monk

**Bhikkhuni** ordained Buddhist nun

**Bible** Christian holy scriptures containing the Old and New Testament; name used for the Jewish Tenakh (which Christians call the Old Testament)

**Bimah** platform from where the holy Torah is read in the synagogue

**Bishop** senior member of the Church priesthood in Anglican, Roman Catholic and Orthodox Churches

**Bodhisattva** one who delays Buddhahood in order to help others

**Brahmacharya** student stage of life, first of the four stages of life in Hindu tradition

**Brahmin** priest, member of the priestly class in traditional Hindu caste system

**Breaking of Bread** see Eucharist

**Brit Milah** rite of circumcision

## C

**Christening** infant baptism

**Circumcision** surgical removal of the foreskin from the penis

**Confess** when someone accepts responsibility for their wrong doings

**Confirmation** rite in which believer makes firm their faith with promises

**Consecrate** make holy

**Covenant** sacred agreement between God and his people

**Cremation** burning of a corpse to reduce it to ashes

## D

**Day of Judgement** religious belief in a day at the end of time when all people will be judged according to their deeds

**Dedication** service of thanksgiving for birth of a child

**Dhamma** teachings of the Buddha

**Dharma** duty, law, religion, religious duty

**Disciples** close friends and followers of Jesus

**Dukkha** suffering, imperfection

## E

**Eightfold Path** eight teachings of the Buddha on how to live

**Eucharist** thanksgiving service in which Christians remember the last supper Jesus shared with his disciples, also called Holy Communion, Mass, Breaking of Bread, The Lord's Supper

## F

**First Communion** special service to mark the first time a Roman Catholic receives the host in the service of the Mass or Eucharist

**Five Ks** five symbols worn by Sikhs – all beginning with the letter K

**Five Pillars of Islam** five basic rules for living in Islam

**Font** bowl or container for the water used for infant baptism

**Four Noble Truths** the first teachings of the Buddha

## G

**Gayatri mantra** daily prayer for enlightenment recited by Hindus

**Ghee** clarified butter used in Hindu worship

**Granthi** one who leads the worship in the Gurdwara

**Grihastha ashram** householder stage in life, second stage of life in Hindu tradition

**Gurdwara** Sikh place of worship

**Guru** spiritual teacher, religious teacher

**Guru Granth Sahib** Sikh holy scriptures

**Guru Nanak** the first of the Ten Gurus of Sikhism

## H

**Hadith** the sayings of the Prophet Muhammad

**Hafiz** one who can recite the Qur'an from memory

**Hajj** pilgrimage to Makkah

**Halal** fit, lawful, permitted

**Havan** fire ritual used in Hindu worship

**Heaven** place of existence after death when the good and faithful will live in the presence of God

**Hell** place or existence after death when those who have lived evil lives and who have rejected God's forgiveness will be separated from God

**Holy Communion** see Eucharist

**Holy Spirit** the power and presence of God working in the lives of Christians

**Host** wafer representing bread from the last supper

**Huppah** canopy used in Jewish wedding under which the couple stand

### I

**Icons** image, painting or mosaic of saint used in devotion in the Orthodox Church

**Imam** one who leads the prayer at the mosque

**Infant baptism** Christian rite in which a baby is anointed with consecrated water and welcomed into the church in Anglican, Orthodox and Roman Catholic traditions

**Iqamah** call to stand for prayer in Islam

### K

**Kachera** shorts worn by Sikhs. One of the Five Ks

**Kaddish** prayer recited by mourners

**Kamma** action, intentional action

**Kangha** comb worn in the hair by Sikhs. One of the Five Ks

**Kara** steel bracelet worn by Sikhs. One of the Five Ks

**Karah parshad** blessed food shared out at Sikh worship

**Karma** actions, the effects and results of actions

**Kaur** 'princess', name given to Sikh girls at the amrit ceremony

**Kesh** long, uncut hair. One of the Five Ks

**Ketubah** Jewish marriage contract

**Khalsa** community of committed Sikhs

**Khanda** double edged ceremonial sword

**Kirpan** sword, symbol of the sword worn by Sikhs. One of the Five Ks

**Kirtan** Sikh devotional song or hymn

**Kirtan Sohila** Sikh evening prayer

**Kosher** foods permitted by Jewish dietary law

**Kshatriya** warrior or ruling class in traditional Hindu caste system

### L

**Langar** shared meal, community kitchen at the Gurdwara

**Lavan** Sikh marriage ceremony

**Laws of Manu** Hindu scriptures giving guidelines on dharma

**Lay community** community of men and women who are not ordained as priests, monks or nuns

**Lord's Supper** see Eucharist

### M

**Madrasah** Qur'an school

**Mahr** wedding dowry paid by the bridegroom

**Makkah** holy city for Muslims, birthplace of the Prophet Muhammad

**Mass** see Eucharist

**Messianic Age** Jewish belief in a time when God's reign will be established on Earth

**Minaret** tall tower from which the call to prayer is given

**Minister** one who leads the worship in a church

**Minyan** ten adult male Jews, minimum number required for worship in many synagogues

**Mohel** trained surgeon who performs rite of circumcision

**Moksha** liberation from cycle of karma and samsara, union with God

**Mool Mantar** Sikh statement of faith or prayer about God summed up in the words of Guru Nanak

**Mosque** place of prostration, place of prayer

**Mu'adhin** one who calls the faithful to prayer from the minaret at the mosque

**Muhammad** name of the last of God's messengers and prophets according to the Qur'an. Whenever Muslims mention his name they add the words 'peace be upon him'. When written this is sometimes shortened to 'pbuh'

**Mukti** liberation from endless cycle of rebirth and blissful union with God

### N

**Nibbana** 'blowing out', a state of perfect peace

**Night of Forgiveness** a special night of prayer and fasting when Muslims remember the Day of Judgement

### O

**Ordination** rite marking the beginning of a religious way of life, usually involving promises

**Orthodox Church** family of Churches including Greek, Russian and Eastern European Churches. Not Roman Catholic or Protestant Churches

**Orthodox Judaism** traditional branch of Jewish community which affirms the authority of all the commandments rather than selecting ones which suit the time or fashion

### P

**Panj piare** the five pure ones, those initiated into the Khalsa

**Paradise** place of perfect peace and joy where the faithful are rewarded for their good deeds after death

**Priest** one who carries out religious rituals and leads worship

**Purgatory** place or existence after death where those who have repented their sin and accept God's forgiveness are purified in readiness for heaven

**Puja** worship, usually involving offerings at a shrine

### Q

**Qur'an** the Muslim holy scriptures

### R

**Rabbi** teacher, leader in the Jewish community

**Rama** the God Vishnu in human form

**Ramadan** the ninth month of the Islamic calendar, during which fasting is required

**Rebirth** being born again on Earth in a new body

**Reform Judaism** branch of Judaism which affirms the importance of interpreting God's commandments in the light of contemporary religious debate

**Resurrection** the rising from the dead of Jesus Christ

**Rites** religious rituals or ceremonies

**Roman Catholic** branch of Christian Church governed by the Pope

## S

**Sacred Thread ceremony** ritual at the Hindu boy's entrance to the first stage of life – the student stage

**Sadhsangat** the true community or assembly of Sikhs

**Saints** holy people now holding a special place in heaven

**Salah** Muslim set prayer said five times a day. One of the Five Pillars of Islam

**Samskar** rituals marking stages in life cycle

**Sandek** one who holds the baby at Brit Milah, godfather

**Sangha** community of ordained monks and nuns in Buddhism

**Sannyas ashram** the last of the four stages of life in Hindu tradition

**Sannyasin** one who is in the fourth stage of life in Hindu tradition, a wandering holy man

**Shabbat** the day of rest and renewal at the end of the week which starts at sunset on Friday and ends at nightfall on Saturday

**Shahadah** declaration of faith: 'there is no God but Allah and Muhammad is His prophet'

**Shivah** seven days of intense mourning following the burial of a close relation

**Singh** 'lion', name given to Sikh males at the amrit ceremony

**Sufi** Muslim mystic, one who sees the oneness of God in all things

**Synagogue** place of congregation, Jewish place of worship

## T

**Tallit** prayer shawl

**Tefillin** small leather boxes containing the words of the Torah worn by Jewish males during weekday prayers

**Ten Precepts** rules for living in the Sangha accepted at Buddhist ordination

**Tenakh** the law, the prophets and the writings, Jewish Bible

**Three Jewels** the three refuges, the Buddha, Dhamma and the Sangha

**Torah** the first five books of the Jewish bible, the most sacred of Jewish scripture

## U

**Upanayana** the Sacred Thread ceremony

## V

**Vaishya** the merchant and business class in traditional Hindu caste system

**Vanaprastha ashram** retirement, the third stage of life in Hindu tradition

**Vihara** temple

## W

**Waheguru** Wonderful Lord, God

## Y

**Yarhzeit** anniversary of death marked in Jewish community

**Yoga** self discipline in life, exercises to control mind and body

## Z

**Zakah** giving to the poor and needy. One of the Five Pillars of Islam